Joe DiStefano

111 Places
in Queens
That You
Must Not Miss

Photographs by Clay Williams

emons:

© Emons Verlag GmbH
All rights reserved
© all photographs: Clay Williams, except:
Steinway & Sons Factory (ch. 94) – Steinway & Sons/Pol Baril
© Cover motif: private
Edited by Karen E. Seiger
Design: Eva Kraskes, based on a design
by Lübbeke | Naumann | Thoben
Maps: altancicek.design, www.altancicek.de
Printing and binding: CPI – Clausen & Bosse, Leck
Printed in Germany 2017
ISBN 978-3-7408-0020-8

Did you enjoy it? Do you want more?
Join us in uncovering new places around the world on:
www.111places.com

Foreword

Jackie Robinson, Ethel Merman, James Brown, and Archie Bunker have all called Queens home. So did my family up until we moved to Long Island when I was just a year old. Even though I had no memories of Queens, I was fascinated as a boy by the Unisphere, the glittering stainless steel globe that we would pass on the highway on the way back from my grandmother's house in Glendale. As I caught a glimpse of it, my mother would fondly recall attending the 1964 World's Fair with my brothers.

Thirty years later, I returned to my birthplace – after brief flirtations with Brooklyn and Staten Island – and fell in love with the most majestic of New York City's boroughs. Every evening after work I would walk the part of the 7 train route – the International Express – from Jackson Heights to Woodside and explore various cultures: Mexican, Thai, and Filipino to name a few. I was learning why they call Queens "The World's Borough." Thanks to this staggering diversity – more than 160 languages are spoken here – it's possible to experience scores of other cultures with only a Metrocard as your passport.

A mural in Jackson Heights depicts homegrown superhero Spiderman, single-handedly holding aloft a subway car alongside the message, "QUEENS IS THE FUTURE." While that's certainly true, Queens is also steeped in history. Flushing is the cradle of religious freedom in America, and Whitestone was once home to Hollywood elite, while Jamaica Estates is the birthplace of Donald J. Trump, and Fort Tilden was once a nuclear fortified stronghold.

Corona's junkyards embody the borough's scrappy sticktoitiveness, and Big Allis, an immense iconic power plant, symbolizes our fortitude. Little Egypt's El Khaiam hookah bar, Flushing's Ganesh temple, and the hip hop mecca of Run-DMC JMJ Way are but a few of the threads in our glorious multicultural tapestry.

Consider this guidebook an invitation to fall in love with Queens, just like I did.

Joe DiStefano

111 Places

1__ 7 Train

All aboard the International Express

If the Unisphere is a static feat of engineering that has taken on more meaning as Queens has grown to become the most diverse community in the world, then surely the 7 train is a mobile representation of the same concept. Now in its 100th year of operation, the train began its life in 1917 as the IRT Flushing line and was officially designated the 7 train in 1948.

Today, the 7 train cuts a broad swath through dozens of immigrant communities inhabited by people from Ireland to Malaysia. In fact, it's possible to travel and eat your way around the world armed with little more than a Metrocard in lieu of a passport. Begin at Flushing–Main Street, the line's eastern terminus and home to the real Chinatown of New York City, featuring a half-dozen food courts and numerous restaurants.

As you board the train to head west you may notice a plaque declaring the "International Express," a Millennium Trail. In 1999, First Lady Hillary Clinton and US Secretary of Transportation Rodney E. Slater designated 16 National Millennium Trails. The 7 train was honored for being a "metaphor for the migration of all the world's people to America's shores," and is in good company alongside the Underground Railroad and the Lewis and Clark National Historic Trail.

As the 7 train travels eastward, it rumbles above Roosevelt Avenue, passing Citi Field, where a group of fans calling themselves the 7 Line Army gathers to cheer on the New York Mets. At Junction Boulevard, you'll find a largely Ecuadorean enclave, and at 61st Woodside an Irish one. Little Manila centers around the 69th Street stop.

There is no stop that better reflects the moniker International Express than 74th Street–Broadway. There, South Asia meets – and intertwines with – South America, as taco trucks stand outside Tibetan cafés just down the street from Indian incense purveyors and Himalayan tattoo parlors.

Address Main Street and Roosevelt Avenue, Flushing, NY | **Getting there** 7 train to Flushing–Main Street | **Hours** Unrestricted | **Tip** It may not be in Queens, but the Transit Museum store in Grand Central Terminal has a great selection of 7 train gear, including T-shirts and baseball caps (Grand Central Terminal, Shuttle Passage, New York, NY 10001, www.nytransitmuseumstore.com).

2 — Addisleigh Park

An English-style suburb that's home to jazz legends

If you live in New York City then you've no doubt heard of the Jackie Robinson Parkway, which is named for Roosevelt "Jackie" Robinson, the player who broke the color barrier in Major League Baseball in the late 1940s. What you might not know is that the legendary Brooklyn Dodger called Queens – specifically Addisleigh Park, a tiny enclave between St. Albans to the east and Jamaica to the west – home. Many other African-American celebrities, including prizefighter Joe Louis and musicians Ella Fitzgerald, John Coltrane, Lena Horne, James Brown, and Count Basie also lived there.

William "Count" Basie, the legendary jazz band leader, lived at 174-27 Adelaide Road in a slate roofed Medieval Revival house, from 1940 until 1982. James Brown, the Godfather of Soul, resided at 175-19 Linden Boulevard, which features a circular stair tower with a conical roof, from 1962 to the early 1970s.

"Tiny Addisleigh, swanky suburb is home of the nation's richest and most gifted Negroes," a September 1952 issue of *Our World* magazine said in a 12-page feature. It wasn't always so though. Addisleigh Park was initially developed as a white community. In the 1930s and 1940s, racially restrictive covenants were introduced into deeds to prohibit the sale of property to African Americans. During the 1940s the New York State Supreme Court upheld covenants in two suits where homeowners were sued by their neighbors for selling their homes to African Americans. In 1948 these restrictions were struck down in the United States Supreme Court.

In 2011, Addisleigh Park was designated as an historic district, not only for the stately English Tudors and other classic houses set back on landscaped lots that make up the neighborhood, but also because it represented a safe community where African Americans, some famous and some not, first began to enjoy suburban living within New York City.

Address Addisleigh Park is bordered by Sayres Avenue to the north, 180th Street to the west, Linden Boulevard to the south, and Merrick Boulevard to the east | Getting there E train to Jamaica Center–Parsons/Archer then Q42 bus to Addisleigh Park | Hours Unrestricted | Tip A mural underneath the St. Albans Long Island Railroad Station on Linden Boulevard at Montauk Street features many of Addisleigh Park's famous residents, including Count Basie, Ella Fitzgerald, Illinois Jacquet, Thomas "Fats" Waller, and Lena Horne.

3_Afrikan Poetry Theatre

Visit a haven for spoken word and jazz in Jamaica

Afrikan Poetry Theatre is tucked away between a barbershop and a law office. For more than 40 years, this cultural institution, whose exterior is emblazoned with colors yellow and red, has hosted everything from concerts by such jazz legends as bassist Stanley Banks to poetry slams from the Urban Poets Movement.

"The colors yellow and red represent the Yoruba deity Shango, the god of thunder," says Saiku Branch, the Afrikan Poetry Theatre's program director, and son of poet John Watusi Branch. Branch's father founded the Afrikan Poetry Ensemble, a collection of poets, singers, and musicians focused on jazz, African rhythms, and poetry, in 1976. Three years later, he moved the Afrikan Poetry Theatre to its current location where a yellow sign featuring a black spider reads, "The Power of the Word."

That spider is none other than Anansi, a West African deity who is represented as a storyteller. "We call him the original Spiderman," Branch says. "He's a trickster who can get himself out of any situation. That's what the spiderweb stands for: the power of the word because it's all about poetry, you know."

Branch has many fond memories of the Last Poets, rap / spoken word pioneers, performing there when he was just a young boy. "They were the first to put poetry over music. These guys were like my uncles," he says. The Afrikan Poetry Theatre along with Manhattan's Nuyorican Poets Café played a big role in the explosion of open mic poetry slams from the 1970s to the 1990s. Danny Simmons, founder of Def Poetry Jam, and the older brother of rapper Joseph "Reverend Run" Simmons of Run-D.M.C. did his first poetry reading at the theater.

These days the theater is as community-oriented as ever, offering free film and acting classes. "We have events where you can play an instrument and then the next person can come on stage and tell you about how their day was," Branch says.

Address 176-03 Jamaica Avenue, Jamaica, NY 11432, +1 (718) 523-3312, www.theafrikanpoetrytheatre.org, afrikanpoetrytheatre@gmail.com | Getting there F train to 179th Street Station | Hours See website for performance schedule and tickets | Tip For West African clothing, including *boubous* and kaftans as well as African dashikis, check out the West African Store (162-10 Jamaica Avenue, Suite 3-6, Jamaica, NY 11432).

4 Albatross Bar

Life's a drag at this Astoria watering hole

"It's like the Super Bowl in here," Nathan Finnegan, owner of Albatross Bar says of the raucous vibe during Friday night of Pride Weekend at his bar, which also coincides with the final episode of RuPaul's Drag Race. The scores of young gay men packing the house and cheering for their favorite drag queens have no shortage of enthusiasm. During commercials the emcee, the redheaded Gilda Wabbit, done up in a tight sequined dress, and her partner in crime, Gloria Swansong, clad in a flower aqua wrap and blonde permanent wave wig, regale the audience. "This is my shortest skirt in my collection," Gilda says. "I have tucked away everything for you so tightly tonight."

Afterwards, the two put on a post-Drag Race drag show of their own, with Gilda channeling Tim Curry's Frank N. Furter as she gyrates and vamps her way through "Sweet Transvestite." Gloria becomes Julia Sugarbaker in a spot-on tirade from Designing Women and does a lip sync of The Scissor Sisters' club favorite "Let's Have a Kiki."

You don't have to wait until Pride Weekend to take in a drag show at Albatross. The oldest LGBTQ bar in Queens stages drag shows hosted by resident drag queen Sutton Lee Seymour every Saturday at 11pm. Performers have included Cacophony Daniels, who played Frankie Valli in Jersey Boys. "They all have amazing voices," Finnegan says of the drag queens who perform at Albatross.

When Finnegan, a straight former aerospace engineer who caught the nightlife bug, took over Albatross two years ago he instituted theme nights, including Brokeback Bingo on Mondays, Show Tuesday Request karaoke on Tuesdays, and regular karaoke on Wednesdays. The bar also hosts viewing parties for the Tony Awards and the Oscars.

What makes Albatross unique, Finnegan says, is its unpretentious neighborhood vibe. "They call it the Cheers of Astoria. It's the opposite of a scene."

Address 36-19 24th Avenue, Astoria, NY 11103, +1 (718) 204-9707, www.albatrossastoria.com, albatrossbarastoria@gmail.com | Getting there N or W train to Astoria Boulevard | Hours Mon–Sat 5pm–4am, Sun 1pm–4am | Tip If karaoke is really your thing, then put your singing skills to the test at Karaoke Shout (32-46 Steinway Street, Astoria, NY 11103, www.karaokeshout.com).

5__All The Right

Queens attitude and street style in Corona

With dozens of T-shirts, caps, high-end jeans, limited edition Nike sneakers, and photos of hip-hop royalty lining the walls, All The Right looks like any other street wear boutique at first. Upon closer scrutiny, however, you'll see that George Landin's shop is really an homage to hip-hop culture, including graffiti. A white sneaker tagged with "All The Right" by Bronx graffiti legends Tats Cru sits atop the counter, which is lined with Molotow brand acrylic markers in every color of the rainbow and black sketch books emblazoned with the shop's logo.

Graffiti legends are everywhere – even on the ceiling. Look up to find a museum of sorts on the ceiling tiles. Landin's favorites include Bronx artists Seen and BG183, both of Tats Cru. Artists Trap and Dio are also represented. There's even a tile devoted to Shiro from Japan, an artist who splits her time between Japan and New York City. "Oh man that took me like 10 years," the 46-year-old Landin said recalling that each artist took a tile home.

Landin, who grew up in nearby Lefrak City, started his Corona shop as a record store in 1998. The name "All The Right" was meant to imply that the shop stocked "all the right records." Landin, who counts Queens' own Run-D.M.C. among his favorite rappers, stopped selling vinyl in 2002.

"Fashion and graffiti are all in one, it's all the same thing. It's a culture," Landin says of his shop whose unique combination of grafitti gear and hip-hop couture draws people from all over, including rap royalty like Nikki Minaj, French Montana, and producer Clark Kent.

"A lot of people talk about Brooklyn and Manhattan, but what about Queens?" Landin says gesturing to a wall outside that features his home borough's name in a rainbow of block letters and Winnie the Pooh styling in a Supreme baseball cap. "I kind of try to rep Queens as hard as I can because Queens is kind of a slept on borough."

Address 91-30 Corona Avenue, Elmhurst, NY 11373, +1 (718) 899-7685, www.alltheright.com, info@alltheright.com | **Getting there** 7 train to 90th Street–Elmhurst Avenue | **Hours** Mon & Tue noon–9pm, Thu–Sat 11am–9pm, Sun noon–7pm | **Tip** After shopping for the latest hip-hop fashion and graffiti gear stop by El Pequeño Coffee Shop for some Ecuadorean cuisine (86-10 Roosevelt Avenue, Jackson Heights, NY 11372, www.elpequeno.nyc).

6 __ Alley Pond Giant

Take a trek to find the king of the forest

Not far from the corner of East Hampton Boulevard and the Horace Harding Expressway in a remote part of Queens known as Oakland Gardens, the king of Queens' trees holds court among mighty oaks and lesser saplings. The Alley Pond Giant, which stands at 133 feet tall and 18 feet in circumference, isn't an oak though. It's a flowering tulip tree estimated to be between 350 and 450 years old.

At the corner just at the entrance to Alley Pond Park is a sign that reads "Forever Wild." Next to it, there's a plaque detailing the tree's vital statistics. You might be tempted to think the mighty tree is next to the sign, but it's not. To find what's reputed to be the oldest living organism in New York City, you'll need to delve deeper. Like many of the best things in Queens, this giant requires some effort to find.

Walk down the paved trail, and about five feet past the end of the black fence head into the woods on your left. Tread carefully on the overgrown trail and be sure to wear good walking shoes or better yet, hiking boots, as it is somewhat steep. At first you might find it hard to see the giant for the forest, but press on, and soon your destination will be in sight. You'll know it by the 8-foot high chain-link fence surrounding it. The elder statesman of the forest, which has borne witness to everything from the Matinecock people treading softly under its boughs to a tour of what was then called Long Island by George Washington in 1790, bears no other marking.

As you look up at the long trunk, which diverges into several zig-zagging branches, it's hard not to feel an overwhelming sense of nature's majesty. You might also feel an urge to hop the fence and stand in the man-sized hollow at the tree's base, but please don't. The fence is there so that this majestic tulip tree can live to the ripe old age of 600 years and bear witness to even more history.

Address East Hampton Boulevard and Horace Harding Expressway, Oakland Gardens, NY 11364 | **Getting there** By car: exit 30, East Hampton Boulevard on the Long Island Expressway; by bus from Midtown Manhattan: QM 5 Glen Oaks bus from Sixth Avenue and West 45th Street to Horace Harding Expressway and 231st Street | **Hours** Open 24 hours daily | **Tip** All that hiking has probably made you hungry, so stop by Grimaldi's for a coal-oven pizza (42-02 61st Avenue, Douglaston, NY 11362, www.grimaldis-pizza.com).

7 __ Anable Basin Sailing Bar & Grill

Dining with skyline views – at an old oil refinery

Much of Long Island City's gritty industrial past, from oil refineries of the 1800s to the light manufacturing of the 20th century, has given way to gleaming residential high-rises. You'll find a vestige of the past, the word "SABOROSO," which means "tasty" in Portuguese, atop a building on the East River and 44th Drive, which was once home to a tropical juice bottling plant. It's especially apt because these days it's home to Anable Basin Sailing Bar & Grill, which boasts some of the tastiest views of the Midtown Manhattan skyline in Queens.

The menu includes a Brazilian *picanha* steak served with the traditional accompaniment of toasted manioc flour known as *farofa*, and *cevapi*, skinless Bosnian sausages served with *ajvar*, a zesty red pepper relish. This culinary diversity is partly an homage to Anable's location in the World's Borough, but it's also a tip of the hat to owner Veso Buntic's heritage. "That's what we eat where I'm from in Herzevogina," said Buntic, who opened Anable in 2008.

The artificial inlet was created in 1868 when the neighborhood was better known for oil refineries than luxury towers and is named for Henry Sheldon Anable, a prominent local politician who was instrumental in the incorporation of Long Island City.

In addition to magnificent sunsets and the twinkling lights of the Queensboro Bridge, Anable Basin features a mural by Italian street artist Blu Muto. You might think the giant yellow gears are a tribute to the industrial past, but a closer look reveals that what Muto has depicted is a printing press spitting out $100 bills. The piece, commissioned in 2010, was inspired by the Federal Reserve bailout of the banks.

"It's one of the only places in the city where you can come dock your boat and have dinner and drinks," says Buntic.

Address 4-40 44th Drive, Long Island City, NY 11101, +1 (646) 207-1333, www.anablebasin.com, anablebasin@ymail.com | Getting there E train to Court Square–23rd Street | Hours Mon–Fri 4:30pm–2am, Sat & Sun 11:30–2am | Tip From the 1940s until 2003 the now landmarked Pepsi-Cola sign sat atop a bottling plant on the other side of the basin. These days, you can see the glowing red cursive letters in nearby Gantry Plaza State Park (30-99 48th Avenue, Long Island City, NY 11101, www.parks.ny.gov).

8 ___ Archie Bunker House

Home of America's most beloved TV bigot

Thirty years before Kevin James played a lovable lug in *The King of Queens*, Carroll O'Connor made the borough famous by playing a lovable bigot from Astoria named Archie Bunker in Norman Lear's groundbreaking sitcom, *All in the Family*.

The pilot, created in 1968 and called *Justice for All* after the names of husband and wife Archie and Edith Justice, never aired. When the show hit the small screen on CBS three years later, its name and the surname of its lead characters had changed, but one thing remained the same: the opening credits feature the couple singing "Those Were the Days," as a bird's-eye view of New York City unfolds, ultimately landing on a stretch of semi-detached homes, and coming to rest at 704 Hauser Street. Archie's malapropisms, frank bigotry, telling his wife to "stifle" herself, and his frustration with a rapidly changing world, would also remain part of the show.

As any Queens resident can quickly tell you, there's something fishy about the address 704 Hauser. It's lacking the dash and two numbers that are the hallmark of all the borough's addresses. There is no Hauser Street in Astoria. Nevertheless, the opening was filmed not in Astoria but on Cooper Avenue in Glendale. Fifty years later, the house still stands at 89–70 Cooper Avenue. Lear came across the block while en route to the airport. As for the street name, his Los Angeles production studio was located near Hauser Street.

Mickey Rooney and Jackie Gleason were both considered for the role of Archie, but ultimately the part went to O'Connor, who grew up in Forest Hills. O'Connor helped give the show local flavor by adding such elements as the fact that Archie was a graduate of Flushing High School.

"It's the best part I've ever played," O'Connor recalled in an interview with the Archive of American Television. "I don't think I'll ever find as good a part as that."

Address 89-70 Cooper Avenue, Glendale, NY 11374 | **Getting there** E train to Forest Hills—71st Avenue; Q23 bus to Metropolitan Avenue/Trotting Course Lane | **Hours** Unrestricted from outside | **Tip** The vast St. John's Cemetery (www.ccbklyn.org/our-cemeteries/saint-john) sits across from the Archie Bunker House, but nearby you'll find a much tinier, much older graveyard, Remsen Cemetery. It's the final resting place of Colonel Jeromus Remsen who fought in the Battle of Long Island and died in 1790 (Trotting Course Lane and Alderton Avenue, www.nycgovparks.org/parks/remsen-family-cemetery/map).

9 __ Artopolis

Greek pastry and culture, Astoria style

Transport your taste buds to Greece with a visit to Artopolis, arguably New York City's best Greek pastry shop. *Arto* means bread and *polis* means city in Greek, says Regina Katopodis, who opened the shop with her husband Angelos Katopodis in 2003. While the store does sell *tsoureki*, a braided Easter bread, it's so much more than a city of bread, offering dozens of traditional Greek cookies, pastries, and 10 types of baklava.

Just inside the entrance is a display piled high with *kourambiethes*, butter cookies made with almonds and Greek brandy. "They're present at all celebrations of life, if a baby is born or a couple gets married or engaged," Katopodis says, "these cookies are always made by the wife in celebration." Another display case is given over to *melomakarona* – honey dipped treats made with walnuts and scented with cinnamon and clove. This star of Artopolis is quite popular during Christmas and New Year.

Among the traditional cookies, you'll find *musto* and almond biscotti, made with a syrup prepared from wine lees, or yeast cells remaining after wine ferments. These, Katopodis says, are traditionally served after funerals. Cretan *diples*, fried sheets of folded dough scented with orange and lemon, grace the tables at wedding and baptism feasts. "I could tell you a story about every single thing that we make," Katopodis says.

Beyond the pastries, breads, and confections, one of the most interesting stories about Artopolis is that everything in the shop, from the baking pans to the glass in the windows, was imported from Greece. "You're literally standing on Athenian marble," Katopodis says.

No visit to Artopolis is complete without a frappe, a traditional Greek iced coffee. "What Greek doesn't like a frappe?" Katopodis asks. "It's more or less like a coffee malted." The matriarch of Artopolis takes hers with milk and "just a splash of sugar."

Address Agora Plaza, 23-18 31st Street, Astoria, NY 11105, +1 (718) 728-8484 | Getting there N or Q train to Astoria–Ditmars Boulevard | Hours Mon–Fri 7am–9pm, Sat & Sun 8am–9pm | Tip Delve deeper into Greek culture with a visit to St. Demetrios Cathedral (30-11 30th Drive, Astoria, NY 11102, www.saintdemetriosastoria.com/church).

10 Batteries at Fort Tilden

Military fortress reclaimed by nature

Signs on the way to the shore at Fort Tilden today read, "Unprotected Beach. No Lifeguards." But from 1917 until 1974, this beach was one of the most protected places in Queens. As one of the most fortified US Army bases on the East Coast, Fort Tilden housed artillery batteries capable of firing 2,100 pound shells a distance of 25 miles. Nuclear-armed Nike missiles, stood at the ready, from the mid-1950s until 1974. They were placed on alert the day after JFK was assassinated.

Battery Harris East, a hulking concrete structure now overtaken by greenery, rises out of the landscape. If you're a birder or just looking for a good view, head up to the observatory deck for sweeping vistas of Jamaica Bay.

Further west, find Battery Harris West, which, like its twin, once housed 16-inch antiaircraft guns. At one time, all of the long-range guns at Fort Tilden were capable of firing 360 degrees. Right before World War II, they were all casemated, or covered in concrete and dirt.

About a 10-minute walk west of the boardwalk, you'll find Battery Kessler rising out of the dunes like something from Planet of the Apes. The central corridor is covered in graffiti, and the darkened antechambers that once stored munitions are truly creepy. Look for the one with a skull painted on the wall.

Fort Tilden was established in 1917 as Camp Rockaway Beach, but the military had recognized its strategic significance a century earlier during the War of 1812, when a blockhouse was built there. By the 1950s, the once state-of-the-art antiaircraft guns proved insufficient to defend against jet airplanes, and nuclear missiles were acquired. With the end of the Cold War, the Army transferred the fort to the National Park Service. Today, the only things being protected at the fort are the fragile ecosystem of the dunes and downy baby shore birds no larger than the palm of your hand.

Address 169 Breezy Point Boulevard, Breezy Point, NY 11697, +1 (718) 338-3799, www.nyharborparks.org/visit/foti.html | Getting there 2 or 5 train to Avenue H/Flatbush Avenue then Q35 bus to Marine Parkway/Rockaway Point Boulevard | Hours Daily dawn–dusk | Tip The 9/11 Tribute Park is dedicated to the memory of those who lost their lives on September 11, 2001. It has a gazebo covered with stained glass inscribed with the names of 70 Rockaway Park residents who were killed in the terrorist attacks on the World Trade Center (Beach 116 Street and Beach Channel Drive, Belle Harbor, NY 11694, www.nycgovparks.org/parks/tribute-park).

11 Beach 97 Street Concessions

Enjoy international eats steps away from the surf

It's a safe bet that when Queens-based punk rock progenitors The Ramones first sang "We can hitch a ride to Rockaway Beach," they never imagined a day when they could dine on Peruvian ceviche while watching the waves. Back then, the boardwalk around Beach 97 Street was better known for the Atom Smasher wooden roller coaster than gourmet beach food.

These days, the concession stand offers a roster of cuisines almost as diverse as Queens itself, including New England lobster rolls from Lobster Joint; brisket from Breezy's BBQ; *salteñas*, or Bolivian empanadas, from The Bolivian Llama Party; Uzbek kebab platters from Uma's; Peruvian ceviche from La Cevicheria; and Colombian arepas made with quinoa and chia from Palenque. There are even San Francisco Mission-style burritos from Super Burrito.

Alcoholic refreshments in the form of sangria slushies can be had at Low Tide Bar. La Fruteria, whose surfboard sign is flanked by two disco balls, features smoothies in such blends as wild blueberry, peach, and banana as well as breakfast sandwiches.

For dessert, visit Citysticks Parlor, which specializes in tropical fruit popsicles, ice cream, and such over-the-top creations as the Flaming S'more Shake, an Oreo Milkshake, topped off with a s'more that's torched before your very eyes.

Afterwards, snap a souvenir photo at a novelty photo cutout. Poke your head through to become either a bikini clad surfer chick hoisting a board that reads "Rockaway Beach," or be her frolicking dog. In addition to referencing the nearby surf beach at 90th Street, the artist has paid homage to another Queens institution, Oswaldo "Miss Colombia" Gomez. Represented by a bearded gent in a floral dress with a parrot, he's a popular sight in Jackson Heights.

Address Beach 97 Street and the Boardwalk | Getting there F train to Roosevelt
Avenue–Jackson Heights then walk to Broadway and 75th Street and take Q 53
bus to Rockaway Beach Boulevard and Beach 98th Street | Hours Mon–Fri noon–6pm,
Sat & Sun 11am–8pm | Tip Rockaway Beach Surf Shop, New York City's oldest surf shop,
predates the Rockaway renaissance by 30 years and offers surfboards handmade by owner
Tom Sena (177 Beach 116th Street, Rockaway Beach, NY 11694, +1 (718) 474 9345,
www.rockawaybeachsurfshop.net).

12_Big aLICe Brewing Co.

Microbrews in the shadow of a major power plant

Just off Vernon Boulevard in Long Island City lies a little brewery named after a big power plant. Big aLICe Brewing Co., which boasts a tap room with 14 draught beers, takes its name from the nearby Ravenswood No. 3 power plant, affectionately known as Big Allis, after the Allis-Chalmers Corporation that built it.

"We don't capitalize the A – we capitalize the LIC in the middle," said Kyle Hurst, one of the co-founders and head brewer. "It's a little nod to our neighborhood." When the brewery opened in 2013, he and his partners were struggling to come up with a name. "We were meeting in the shadow of the power plant, and we asked, 'What the heck is this thing called?'" Hurst recalls. When they found out it was called Big Allis, they fell in love with the name. "You can see those smokestacks from most anywhere in Queens," he says. "Look for Big Allis, and you'll find us a couple of blocks away."

Big aLICe started small with a 10-gallon brewing system. Today a photo of that original system hangs on the wall. Next to it is a roster of the first 141 beers Big aLICe ever brewed. The first was a red ale with pumpkin. All beer making is still done on site in the adjacent brewhouse, which sports five gigantic stainless-steel brewing kettles. Don't be surprised if you stop in for a pint and find the bar area suffused with the toasty aroma of malt along with coriander and orange, as the brewing schedule often overlaps with the tap room's hours.

The brewery's name isn't the only thing that pays homage to the neighborhood. There's a stout called "LIC Native," that's made with coffee from Astoria's Native Roasters. "Date Night, Bro?" is another stout that combines coffee with donuts in a drinkable tribute to the NYPD. "We try to focus on keeping things creative and interesting but drinkable because you can go off the deep end pretty quickly," Hurst says.

Address 8-08 43rd Road, Long Island City, NY 11101, +1 (347) 688-2337,
www.bigalicebrewing.com, info@bigalicebrewing.com | **Getting there** Subway 7, E, G, or
M train to Court Square | **Hours** See website for details | **Tip** Continue your exploration of
Queens' burgeoning beer scene with a visit to Rich Castagna's Bridge and Tunnel Brewery
(15-35 Decatur Street, Ridgewood, NY 11385, www.bridgeandtunnelbrewery.com).

13 Big Allis

Behold the power of Queens

You'll find her on the corner of 37th Avenue and Vernon Boulevard in a sliver of Long Island City known as Ravenswood. Her name is Big Allis. Her quartet of red-and-white smokestacks tower over the neighborhood and are visible around every corner. Look down Vernon Boulevard at dusk, and you'll see her stacks lazily emitting puffs of steam as the blinking red lights on top turn on in sequence. Formally known as Ravenswood No. 3, the gigantic power plant has become a symbol of Long Island City over the years.

The stacks may be colloquially referred to as "Big Allis," but really that name belongs to the largest of the power plant's three turbines, a million kilowatt unit that was the largest in the world at the time of its construction by Allis-Chalmers. Con Edison, which commissioned the plant, had originally intended to construct a nuclear power plant on the site, which once housed the East River Gas Company.

You won't be able to get inside Ravenswood No. 3 to get a peek at Big Allis herself, nor would you really want to. The turbine is as noisy as a jet engine and the temperatures inside typically sit at 160 degrees Fahrenheit. Water is heated in a gigantic boiler generating steam that spews forth at a pressure of 2,400 pounds per square inch, spinning the gigantic blades of the turbine, which in turn rotate the stator, thus generating electricity.

Not only is Big Allis iconic in the neighborhood, in 1997 it played a role in the Mel Gibson film, *Conspiracy Theory*, as the headquarters of a nefarious government mind-control program. These days the plant is no longer owned by Con Edison, but it continues to generate between 20 and 25 percent of all electricity consumed in New York City. Visible from five miles away in Forest Hills with the Manhattan skyline in the background, the red-and-white stacks symbolize the power of Queens itself as well as the fortitude of the men and women who toil away to provide electricity for the city's residences and businesses.

Address 37-20 37th Avenue, Long Island City, NY 11101 | **Getting there** F train to 21st Street–Queensbridge, head northeast on 21st Street toward 40th Avenue, turn left onto 40th Avenue, turn right onto Vernon Boulevard | **Hours** Unrestricted, viewable from the outside only | **Tip** Named for Dr. Thomas Rainey, one of the men who helped to envision the Queensboro Bridge, Rainey Park, an oasis amidst otherwise industrial Ravenswood, is perfect for a picnic (Vernon Boulevard and 34th Avenue, Astoria, NY 11106, www.nycgovparks.org/parks/rainey-park-q048).

14__Bowlero Queens

Old school fun at lanes with a modern twist

Despite the fact that bowling plays a major role in the TV show *The King of Queens*, there are few places in the borough left to engage in the sport that smacks of Americana and rented shoes.

Woodhaven Lanes, the old-school bowling alley that was once the pride of Glendale, Hollywood Lanes in Rego Park, Americana Lanes in Ozone Park, and Cameo Bowling Casino in Forest Hills, have all been shuttered for more than a decade. Nevertheless, bowling is still alive and well – with a modern update of black lights and large-screen TVs – at Bowlero in Woodside.

You'll find the modern take on the classic 1950s institution just off the Brooklyn–Queens Expressway. Outside, Bowlero sports a classic red diamond motif and a retro script logo that harkens back to the days of James Dean and tailfins. Inside, you'll find 35 lanes of bowling lit up by black lights plus billiards, shuffleboard, and air hockey.

After you've found the perfect ball and hopefully thrown a few strikes while taking in a concert or live sports on the screens that form the background of the alleys, you might start to feel the need for sustenance. No need to head over to the snack bar. At Bowlero, the snack bar comes to you. The ultramodern recreation specialist offers laneside service for both food and beverages, which include a chilled tower of Pabst Blue Ribbon beer and such cocktails as the colorful Mad Mai Tai, a festive concoction of Sailor Jerry Rum, Disaronno Originale, pineapple juice, and a float of Bacardi Black. Oh, and if the players really need to imbibe, you can all head over to the bar and order a classic White Russian.

Food offerings include such classic pub – and bowling alley – grub as pizza, burgers, wings, mozzarella sticks, nachos, and fries. When you and your crew are feeling especially hungry, you won't want to miss the Behemoth Burger, a five-pound, 14-inch round party burger with bacon, American cheese, pickles, tomatoes, lettuce, and special sauce.

Address 69-10 34th Avenue, Woodside, NY 11377, +1 (718) 651-0440, www.bowlero.com/location/bowlero-queens | **Getting there** R train to 65th Street Station | **Hours** Mon & Tue noon–midnight, Wed & Thu noon–11pm, Fri noon–1am, Sat & Sun 11am–11pm | **Tip** Try your hand at a decidedly different game – snooker – at Weekender Billiard alongside Nepalese expats who are crazy about the game (41-46 54th Street, Woodside, NY 11377).

15 Broadway Silk Store

The fabric of family tradition

Sandwiched between an Eastern European butcher and a Thai restaurant is the Broadway Silk Store, a shop that offers a glimpse into a simpler, more homespun time. During the Great Depression, this family-owned fabric store specialized in silk. "At one time, silk stores were the best," says Pearl Gould, Broadway Silk's matriarch, who still comes to work at the age of 87. "We used to sell only silk, cotton, and rayon, but my daughter brought in the other things. She's my guiding light."

Those other things that her daughter, Sarah-Beth White, added include vintage-inspired jewelry, decorative knick-knacks, and handicrafts from local artists. There's less silk these days, but still plenty of fabric, from linens, wools, and satins to scores of cotton prints with whimsical designs, cats, an array of handbags and heels, and one bearing the words Hope, Peace, Love, and Joy. "They used to be 29 cents a yard. Now they're $5 a yard," Pearl says, gesturing to the shelves of fabric. "My job was to double the fabric onto those bolts. We still do that."

The shelves and wooden counters were built by Sarah-Beth's great-uncle, Ellie Laxer, a carpenter who founded the shop more than 80 years ago with his wife Esther. Some of his tools, including saws with ornate carved handles, still hang at the back. Other antiques line the counter, including a needlepoint of the word "America," which Pearl made as a little girl. "Lots of people think we sell antiques, but they're for decoration," Sarah-Beth says.

Broadway Silk has even had a few brushes with fame. Artists from Sesame Street, which is filmed at nearby Kaufmann Astoria Studios, and upholsterers from The Cosby Show have shopped there. Pearl recalls how she would watch for her fabric to appear on couches and chairs on the shows. These days, customers are a mix of older seamstresses and the younger DIY crowd.

Address 35-11 Broadway, Astoria, NY 11106, +1 (718) 728-2519, broadwaysilks@gmail.com | Getting there M or R train to Steinway Street | Hours Daily 11:30am–6pm | Tip After shopping for arts and craft supplies take a break with craft beer and cheese at nearby Astoria Bier & Cheese, which sells exactly what they advertise (34-14 Broadway, Astoria, NY 11106, www.astoriabierandcheese.com).

16__Brooklyn Grange

State-of-the-art rooftop farming in LIC

The name might lead you to believe it's located in Kings County, but the world's largest rooftop soil farm is actually in Queens. Perched atop the Standard Motor Products building, the farm in the sky supplies such New York City temples of gastronomy as Gramercy Tavern and Balthazar. The farm boasts sweeping vistas of the New York City skyline and Queens landmarks Big Allis and Hellgate Bridge.

By early summer, the one-acre rooftop farm is a sea of salad greens: arugula, baby mustards, kale, and several types of romaine lettuce, including dark purple varieties high in antioxidants. "My favorite is a type called *forellenschluss* or Amish speckled lettuce," says Brooklyn Grange co-founder and vice president Anastasia Cole Plakias. "It's Pennsylvania Dutch German for speckled trout tail. It's very delicious and very sweet."

When Cole founded Brooklyn Grange in 2010 with president Ben Flanner, the two thought the farm was going to be in Brooklyn. A real estate deal fell through, and so the farm moved atop a building with a gigantic wooden water tank that was to become the farm's logo. However, the tank is not used to water the farm's herbs and hot peppers. Water for the crops comes from inside. Those herbs and peppers, including Peruvian *aji dulce* peppers, are used to make Brooklyn Grange hot sauce. "It's Ben's secret recipe," Cole says.

Every Saturday from mid-May through October, you'll find a farmers' market underneath the water tower. It's also a day that the Brooklyn Grange opens itself up to the public. "You can jump in alongside our farm team and get your hands dirty, or you can just simply come up and enjoy the green space," Cole says.

The farm offers private tours, and several dinners, including a pig pickin' and crawfish boil, are held throughout the summer. It also runs a CSA (community supported agriculture) program where members pick up produce weekly.

Address 37-18 Northern Boulevard, Long Island City, NY 11101, +1 (347) 670-3660, www.brooklyngrangefarm.com, info@brooklyngrangefarm.com | Getting there M or R train to 36th Street | Hours May 20–Oct 21 Sat 11am–4pm, tours may be signed up for on website as well | Tip Start a farm of your own with a visit to Hydroponic Garden Centers (127-11 20th Avenue in College Point, NY 11356, www.growhome.com).

17_Butala Emporium

Explore the many facets of Indian culture

You'll feel as if you've traveled half way around the world when you open the doors to this 20-year-old shop specializing in Indian and South Asian goods. From cosmetics to cricket bats to dozens of varieties of incense and cookware, if it comes from India you'll find it at this two-level emporium in the heart of Jackson Heights.

Hindu hymns are often playing, and garlands of flowers hang from the ceiling. An entire aisle is devoted to statues of Hindu gods and historical figures, including Gandhi. In the basement of the shop, whose motto is "Keeping Traditions Alive," are gigantic statues of Ganesh and other devas that bear $2,000+ price tags.

When Bhadra Butala came to America from Gujarat in 1989, his shop consisted of little more than a table lined with books and magazines from India. After running the smaller shop, the Butala family moved their store to its current location in 1998.

"We have merchandise from every corner of India from South, West, East, North," notes Bhadra's son, Shashwat, who manages the Jackson Heights store. Brass statues and fabrics used to clothe the gods in temples are sourced from northern India, while fine carvings and ceramics come from Calcutta in the south.

The shop still sells many of the same magazines and horoscope guides at the front of the store with which the Butala family started its business. Butala offers an extensive selection of Indian comic books from Amar Chitra Katha that tell tales of the Hindu gods – Ganesh, Krishna, Vishnu, and more – and historical and religious figures, including Gandhi and Jesus Christ. There are also hundreds of other books and magazines ranging from titles on spirituality, to Punjabi-English dictionaries, and cookbooks. An entire aisle is devoted to Indian cookware, such as ghee pots and brass mortar and pestles, as well as stainless-steel tiffin lunch boxes and copper cooking vessels.

Address 37-46 74th Street, Jackson Heights, NY 11372, +1 (718) 899-5590, www.indousplaza.com, service@indousplaza.com | **Getting there** Subway 7, E, F, M, or R train to Jackson Heights–Roosevelt Avenue | **Hours** Daily 10am–8:30pm | **Tip** After shopping at Butala for cookbooks and kitchenware, head directly across the street to Patel Brothers, a vast Indian supermarket with all manner of ingredients (37-27 74th Street, Jackson Heights, NY 11372, www.patelbros.com).

18_Carlo Gambino's Grave

Where the Mafia "boss of all bosses" rests in peace

With its stone walls and tall, narrow windows, the five-story St. John's Cloister bears more than a passing resemblance to a penitentiary. Lying within the cemetery of the same name, the cloister's prison-like appearance is especially apt, since one of its most infamous residents is Carlo Gambino, the Mafia *capo di tutti capi* ("boss of all bosses") who helped to inspire Don Vito Corleone, the central figure in *The Godfather*.

Like the fictional Corleone, real-life gangster Gambino died quietly at home in Massapequa, NY on October 15, 1976. Gambino, who at the time of his death ruled over what was then the richest and most powerful Mafia family in the United States, was laid to rest in a $7,000 bronze coffin the day after a fatal heart attack.

You'll find his family mausoleum on the fifth floor of St. John's Cloister. You might feel a sense of both peace and creepiness, your footsteps on the marble floor echoing as you pass dozens of the deceased while Catholic hymns play in the background. Once in Section 2, you won't have too much trouble finding the Gambino mausoleum.

Don Carlo's tomb is just above his wife Kathryn's. The small room is decorated by a stained-glass panel of an angel holding a banner that reads, "Allelluia," and bears the message "Give Glory to the Lord." The stained-glass window depicting the Supper at Emmaus at the end of the hall is worth taking a look at.

Two floors down, you'll find another infamous Mafioso, John Gotti. For a man who was so flashy in life, the final resting place of the "Teflon Don" is surprisingly plain, marked by little more than a polished wooden plaque.

St. John's Cemetery is actually somewhat of a who's who of New York Mafia royalty. In Section 11, you'll find the grave of Vito Genovese. Nearby is a mausoleum with the remains of Joe Profaci, and Salvatore "Lucky Luciano" Lucania rests in Section 3.

Address 80-01 Metropolitan Avenue, Middle Village, NY 11379, +1 (718) 894-4888, www.ccbklyn.org/our-cemeteries/saint-john | **Getting there** 7 train to 69th Street/Roosevelt Avenue then Q47 bus to 80th Street/Juniper Valley Road | **Hours** Daily 8am–5pm | **Tip** For a slightly less morbid slice of Mafia history, check out GoodFellas Diner, formerly the Clinton Diner, where several scenes from the classic film were shot (56-26 Maspeth Avenue, Maspeth, NY 11378, www.facebook.com/GoodFellasDiner).

19___Central Governor

Artistic alchemy in an old boiler room

You'd never expect a 115-year-old boiler room in Long Island City's first schoolhouse to look quite like this one. Enter a brick-lined basement chamber in the MoMA PS1 modern art museum to find Saul Melman's Central Governor, a furnace coated in shimmering gold leaf. The Brooklyn-based artist's work is the culmination of a six-month-long performance piece that was presented in the 2010 *Greater New York* exhibition.

Melman spent three weeks sand-blasting away layers of rust that coated the coal-fired Williams & Greets furnace and tanks, stripping them down to the bare metal. He also cleaned the basement's grimy windows, allowing natural light to suffuse the subterranean space.

Melman, who is also an emergency room doctor, would come to the museum every day clad in a T-shirt depicting the Plague Doctor – an historic figure who dressed in a full-length leather outfit including a leather hat with a beak. Then he'd change into a blue jumpsuit to sweep and tidy the space in between his work chipping away at a 5,000-pound stack of salt blocks. His other role was that of a medieval gilder, clad in a customized long white apron.

In order to learn how to apply the squares of gold leaf, Melman studied with a Red Hook-based master gilder. He used sweat from the back of his neck, which he had coated with vegetable oil, as an adhesive to apply the gold leaf. Melman also used his own saliva. Look carefully for two vials in the center of the piece that contain his bodily fluids.

Central Governor takes its name from a bodily process that safely regulates exercise so that it does not reach a level of intensity where it will damage the heart. It raises the question of how much continued exertion it required on Melman's part to accomplish the alchemy of transforming rusty, abandoned machinery – pipes, tanks, and the furnace itself – into a glittering masterpiece.

Address 22-25 Jackson Avenue, Long Island City, NY 11101, +1 (718) 784-2084, www.momaps1.org, mail_ps1@moma.org | **Getting there** E, G, M, or 7 train to Court Square | **Hours** Thu–Mon noon–6pm | **Tip** Experience modern art of a different kind – desserts designed via 3D printer – at the nearby SugarCube (10-16 50th Avenue, Long Island City, NY 11101, www.sugarcubenyc.com).

20 __ Château Le Woof

Coffee and canines at a French-themed café

It all started with a desire for good, strong coffee and a great love for dogs. Natassa Contini opened the French-themed Château Le Woof Pet Market & Café two years ago, after being unable to find a cup of joe on her morning stroll with her pooch.

Just inside New York City's first pet market / café you'll see a red-and-yellow fire hydrant. Contini salvaged it from nearby Socrates Sculpture Park. Sometimes, she says with a laugh, dogs get confused by the fire plug. "We've had accidents."

"I'd wake up every morning and go for a walk with my dog, searching for a decent cup of coffee," Contini recalls. "I couldn't really find anything nearby, I'd have to walk a good 15 to 20 minutes."

Now she and her neighbors have a place to enjoy La Colombe Workshop Coffee. Hers is the only shop in Queens using the high-end beans. "We brew a different drip – Ethiopian, Mexican, Brazilian, etc. – every week in order for people to get a feel for what they like."

Images of the Eiffel Tower line the walls and French music plays at the café. The logo is a French bulldog named Bonaparte, sporting a jaunty beret. Contini doesn't own a French bulldog, but she has many customers who do.

As befits a French café for canines and their humans, there are macaroons from an organic bakery in Flushing, as well as treats from Astoria's Single Girl Cookies. There are macaroons for dogs in such flavors as coconut limoncello, *naturellement.* The shop stocks a full line of Abady organic dog food in such flavors as lamb, duck, and buffalo. For the *très chic chien*, there's nail polish in hot pink and outfits, like a powder blue rhinestone tutu. On weekends, the Château hosts doggy happy hours from 6pm – 8pm, a special time when pets are allowed to frolic in the shop. Contini doesn't offer coffee for dogs, but she does make a venison and beef bone broth. Think of it as medicinal cold brew for your best friend.

Address 30-02 14th Street, Long Island City, NY 11102, +1 (718) 626-9663, www.chateaulewoof.com, info@chateaulewoof.com | Getting there N or W train to 30th Avenue | Hours Mon–Fri 7am–8pm, Sat & Sun 8am–8pm | Tip After a visit to the château, take your best friend for a stroll through the outdoor Socrates Sculpture Park (32-01 Vernon Boulevard, Long Island City, NY 11106, www.socratessculpturepark.org).

21 _ The Chestnut King

Piping hot Chinese treats on the streets of Flushing

From fall until early summer you'll find New York City's only Chinese roasted chestnut vendor in the heart of downtown Flushing's bustling Chinatown. Unlike the chestnuts sold on the streets of midtown Manhattan, Tianjin *tang chao li zi*, or Tianjin sweet roasted Chinese chestnuts, are smaller, sweeter, and far more delicious than their Western counterparts. In Tianjin, China, *li zi* are quite popular. There's a shop in Tianjin called Li Li Xiang that's been selling the chestnuts for more than 80 years.

The aroma of freshly roasted chestnuts might bring to mind Mel Tormé's soft crooning of "The Christmas Song," but you won't find any open fire at this hawker stand in Flushing. The proprietor, Ken Ren, who hails from Qingdao, and his wife cook the chestnuts in a gas-fired device that tumbles them with hot pebbles, steaming the unshelled delicacies evenly from within. Each year he imports several tons from Tianjin in huge burlap bags. Every now and then Ken's season ends early. "Sometimes there are just no more chestnuts," he says with a laugh.

You might be tempted to bite them open, but there's a much more elegant method to get at the tender, sweet flesh: hold a nut in one hand, with the other run your fingernail down the center of the flat side, and squeeze gently to pop the flesh out. Eat, enjoy, and repeat. If you're having trouble opening your chestnuts, the King will gladly show you how to open one.

The white street cart bears the words "Fresh Roasted Chestnut." Another sign touts their various health benefits: high in vitamin B, good sources of energy, good for metabolism, good for high-blood pressure, and so on. While the jury is out on whether the chestnuts – $12 for a pound, $7 for a half, and $3.50 for a quarter – are a panacea, they are certainly a tasty seasonal treat. The bag makes a fine hand warmer too, yet another benefit to your health.

Address 40th Road just west of Main Street, Flushing, NY 11355, +1 (718) 581-9077 | Getting there 7 train to Flushing–Main Street | Hours Late fall until early summer 10am–9pm | Tip The steps leading up to the Flushing branch of the Queens Borough Public Library are etched with the titles of folk tales from around the world, including China's "Journey to the West," America's "Johnny Appleseed," and Ghana's "Anansi the Spider" (41-17 Main Street, Flushing, NY 11355, www.queenslibrary.org/flushing).

22__Cleansing Biotope
Recreating a wetland to filter rainwater

Before it became home to America's first commercial nursery in 1730 – a legacy that lives on in avenues like Ash and Cherry – much of Flushing was wetland marshes. A small corner has been returned to its prior state. It's called the Cleansing Biotope, and you'll find it at the Queens Botanical Garden (QBG).

The Biotope was inspired by QBG's commitment to environmental stewardship, says Gennadyi Gurman, head of interpretation. Surveys of the public revealed a strong connection to water across every nationality and age group. QBG briefly considered digging up a creek, but deemed it impractical. Thus the Cleansing Biotope was born.

You'll find it to the left of the administration building. Part of it consists of a pond that collects rainwater from the building's pitched roof. "A biotope is a fancy way of saying a big pond where living things survive," Gurman says, adding that when it was first established it filled up with dragon fly nymphs, diving beetles, and snails.

Behind two trees to the left of the administration building is a bioswale lined with geofabric and filled with soil that absorbs water really fast. It's planted with native swamp species like red twigged dogwood that are both really drought resistant and able to survive floods. The ditch fills up with rainwater, and before mosquitoes have a chance to hatch, it's all absorbed into the soil and taken up by the plants, which then transpire it into the atmosphere. "On those really hot days after a summer storm, you get a little bit of a cooling effect," Gurman says.

Some of the collected water goes into a 24,000-gallon cistern, and from there it flows into the Fountain of Life, an amphitheater-shaped water feature just inside the garden's entrance. After bubbling up through the fountain, it flows behind the building and is returned to the biotope, effectively creating a loop where none of the rain-water is lost.

Address 43-50 Main Street, Flushing, NY 11355, +1 (718) 886-3800,
www.queensbotanical.org, info@queensbotanical.org | Getting there 7 train to
Flushing–Main Street | Hours Tue–Sun 8am–6pm | Tip Not far from the garden,
wedged in between a sari shop and a halal butcher, you'll find a storefront temple,
the World Buddhist Ch'an Jing Center (44 Main Street, Flushing, NY 11355,
www.sgs-wbcjc.org/main/en/intro/intro_sgs.php).

23_ The Cliffs LIC

Crush it at this indoor climbing gym

A few blocks away from a canyon of gleaming waterfront towers, you'll find a canyon of a different sort, The Cliffs LIC. This indoor rock climbing gym draws people of all skill levels, from novice to Olympic hopeful.

Red, blue, yellow, and green climbing holds line the walls, which include a 60-foot lead wall, a 45-foot top rope wall, and 16-foot boulder. "It's what it sounds like, climbing large boulders," says Bill Baer the director of the Cliffs LIC. "Instead of it being about climbing great heights you're actually climbing with very difficult moves." In top roping, the rope is secured to the top of the wall and a person on the bottom acts as counterbalance, pulling back should the climber lose their grip. Lead roping involves taking the rope up as you climb and clipping it to carabiners.

Classes are available so don't worry if you don't know an undercling from a hand foot match or have never taken a whipper! Classes include intro to climbing, which covers knots, and belaying and sport lead, which covers catching falls and how to handle a whipper, or a dynamic fall.

"If you walk in with no experience we can help you become a climber," says Baer. A common misconception is that climbing requires a lot of upper body strength. One of the first things you'll learn is how to hang from your skeleton, allowing your biceps and forearms to rest by hanging away from the wall. "You're removing all these extra muscles that aren't needed to hold you there. All you really need are your fingers and your toes."

The bookshelf at the Cliffs LIC is lined with titles like *The Hillwalker's Manual* and *The Climber's Guide to The Shawangunks*. "We have actual rock climbers here who spend most of their time in the mountains," Baer says. "That's what this sport really is based on." Hence the gym's slogan: "Get the skills to get outside."

Address 11-11 44th Drive, Long Island City, NY 11101, +1 (718) 729-7625 | **Getting there** E, G, M, or 7 train to Court Square–23rd Street | **Hours** Mon–Fri 6–midnight, Sat & Sun 9am–10pm | **Tip** Run some laps or check out a soccer game at the nearby Queens West Sportsfield (5th Street between 46th Road and 47th Avenue, Long Island City, NY 11101).

24_ Commonwealth Cricket League

The British pastime is alive and well in Queens

In Corona, men outfitted with balls and bats gather on Sunday afternoons to pursue their national pastime. They hail from Bangladesh, Guyana, India, Trinidad, and Pakistan. They come to test their skills on the three public cricket pitches. The 66-foot-long stretches are home to the Commonwealth Cricket League, which has scores of teams, including the Camelot Cricket Club from Kew Gardens and the Royal Knights from Richmond Hill.

Every Sunday at 1pm from May until early September, the 11-member teams gather in crisp white uniforms to face off. While there are balls, bats, runs, and outs in cricket, that's where the similarity to baseball ends. For one thing, matches last upwards of four hours, with scores ranging well into the hundreds of runs.

Stationed at either end of the pitch are two batsmen. Before taking a whack at the leather-bound ball, the batsman taps his curved bat on the ground. Then the bowler runs up to the line and pitches the ball overhand. If the batted ball hits one of the wickets at the other end or is caught, the batsman is out. If it lands on the infield, the batsmen take turns running between the wickets. If they reach the wicket before a fielder can knock it over with the ball, they score a run. If the ball bounces past the orange cones in the outfield then four runs are scored, and if it passes them on the fly, six runs are scored.

Cricket might seem a genteel sport, but there is trash talk. "Catcher, catch the ball! You can't catch! The only thing you can catch is a cold in the summer."

Playoffs take place in late summer when the US Open is just gearing up nearby. Even if you don't quite understand the rules, watching a game is a fine way to while away an afternoon.

Address Flushing Meadows–Corona Park, Corona, NY 11368, www.commonwealthcricketleague.com | Getting there 7 train to Mets–Willets Point Station, head southeast toward Flushing Meadows Pedestrian Bridge left on New York Avenue, right onto Avenue of Commerce, right onto Meridian Road, left onto Meadow Lake Road West | Hours Mid-May through early Sept Sun 1–5pm | Tip In mid-August, The Hong Kong Dragon Boat Festival brings together more than 120 teams on nearby Meadow Lake (Flushing Meadows Park, www.hkdbf-ny.org).

25 Corona Park Pool and Rink

Swim like an Olympian and skate like a ranger

New York City may have lost its 2012 Olympic bid to London, but Queens still has the 1,250-square-meter Olympic swimming pool and regulation National Hockey League ice skating rink to show for it. You don't have to be an Olympian or a pro hockey player to use them.

Opened in 2008, the Flushing Meadows Corona Park Natatorium and Ice Rink is an architectural masterpiece inspired by the 1939 and 1964 World's Fair pavilions. The sweeping cable-supported canopy roof suspended over the 110,000-square-foot building simultaneously calls to mind a futuristic version of a 19th-century clipper and a suspension bridge. Each 40-ton steel mast soars to 130 feet.

"From a valley of ashes to World's Fairs grounds to a stunning contemporary building with soaring masts – the new Flushing Meadows Corona Park Pool and Ice Rink marks an important milestone in the history of the park and our city," said former New York City Parks Commissioner Adrian Benepe when the complex opened in 2008. Since it was designed with the Olympics in mind, the 1 million gallon pool has seating for 414 spectators. And there's room for even more, as the design allows for the walls running the length of the facility to be removed to expand to a larger venue with a temporary bleacher structure. Three diving boards, one 3-meter and two 1-meter, stand above the 80-degree pool, which goes as deep as 12 feet in the diving area. A glass wall offers a view of the park's flora, including flowering crabapple trees in spring and ruddy maple groves in the fall.

The largest recreational complex in a New York City park also houses the World Ice Arena, which features the Unisphere on its logo. Hockey players, figure skaters, speed skaters, and wobbly first-time ice skaters come to the rink. Classes include private figure skating lessons to ice hockey. You can even have your birthday party here.

Address 131-04 Meridian Road, Flushing, NY 11368, +1 (718) 271-7572, www.nycgovparks.org/parks/flushing-meadows-corona-park | Getting there 7 train to Mets–Willets Point Station | Hours Mon–Fri 6am–9:30pm, Sat 9am–9:30pm, Sun 9am–7:30pm | Tip After some laps and / or double axels, take in some culture at the Queens Museum (New York City Building, Flushing Meadows Corona Park, Corona, NY 11368, www.queensmuseum.org).

26__ Creedmor Psychiatric Center

Do not enter Building 25

Just off the Grand Central Parkway stands one of the creepiest places in New York City: the abandoned Building 25 of Creedmor Psychiatric Center. The front door bears a large red X, denoting that it is unsafe for human habitation. In fact, the only inhabitants of the four-story brick structure abandoned in the 1970s are birds, whose droppings are piled into pungent hillocks on the upper floors. With knocked out windows overrun by vines and an eerie, desolate atmosphere, Building 25 looks like the setting for a horror movie.

Creedmor has borne witness to its own horrors. In 1943, there was an outbreak of dysentery, and in the 1970s, it was plagued with crime and patient abuse. In 1974, Dr. Alan D. Miller, then New York State's Commissioner of Mental Hygiene ordered an investigation after 22 assaults, 52 fires, 130 burglaries, 6 suicides, a shooting, and a riot took place over 20 months. There's no need for zombie stories; the reality was bad enough.

When the Lunacy Commission of New York State opened the center in 1912 as a Farm Colony of Brooklyn State Hospital, it was a bucolic haven. With gymnasiums, a swimming pool, and later a television studio, it served some 7,000 patients who raised livestock and tended gardens. Today, the population has dwindled to mere hundreds, and the only green space is the one that has overtaken Building 25.

Peer through the fence to see an entire corner covered in weeds and benches encased in lichen. The grounds are off limits, but there's a hole in the fence. It's illegal and inadvisable, but those who dare go up to the front door and peer through will see a fallout shelter sign alongside the fallout of abandonment: peeling paint, decaying desks, and rusting hospital equipment. It's not a sight that's easy to forget, just like the dank smell that permeates the grounds.

Address Main Campus is located at 79-25 Winchester Boulevard, Queens Village, NY 11427; Building 25 can be found on the South Campus, which lies just across Union Turnpike. | **Getting there** By car: take I-495 East to Exit 31S for Cross Island Parkway South, take Exit 28B toward Union Turnpike, take Union Turnpike to Winchester Boulevard | **Hours** Viewable from the outside only; Main Campus is open 24 hours | **Tip** In nearby Cunningham Park, find the Vanderbilt Motor Parkway, which began as America's first all-elevated road for cars and was used by fashionable New Yorkers to drive to their weekend homes in Long Island. In 1938, it was transformed into a tree-lined bike path that runs all the way to Jamaica (northwest corner of Winchester Boulevard and Union Turnpike).

27_ The Creek & The Cave

The foundations of comedy and the subway

Colin Quinn, Jerry Seinfeld, and Louis C.K. are not necessarily comics you'd associate with Queens. Yet each has graced the stage at The Creek & The Cave, a Long Island City comedy club tucked into the basement of a Mexican restaurant. Before Rebecca Trent opened the club in 2007, the space hosted raucous reggaeton parties. After realizing the music was driving her neighbors crazy, Trent put her passion for comedy to work. "I grew up watching comedy and memorizing comedy albums," Trent recalls. "I know every word to Dennis Leary's 'No Cure for Cancer.' I know almost every Bill Cosby album by heart."

The club hosts some 150 live performances a month and 20 open mics a week. There's everything from traditional standup and one-person shows to pilot testing for Comedy Central. Homegrown talent Chris Gethard, who got his start on Queens Public Television, developed his Comedy Central show at the club. "A lot of incredible jokes got born here," Trent says.

One of the more unique shows is The Naked Show, a performance that takes place quarterly at 11:59pm. As the name states, comedians do their sets in the buff. "There's a group of about 60 comics who are willing to perform nude," Trent says. The club's website notes the audience "has the option of being as naked as they like! (please come wearing clothes, we will let you know when it's ok to get naked)."

The venue is named for Newton Creek and the original bedrock discovered when the basement was being developed. Every so often, Trent says, she catches a glimpse of "old sandhogs just touching the bricks and kind of licking and testing them to see if they are salty." Sandhogs are the people who build the subways, including the one underneath Long Island City.

Look for the framed cutouts of bedrock in the bar area, which also features a collection of pinball machines, including Trent's favorite, "The Sopranos."

Address 10-93 Jackson Avenue, Long Island City, NY 11101, +1 (718) 706-8783, www.creek.com, creekticketing@gmail.com | Getting there 7 train to Vernon Jackson, G train to 21st Street, E/M train to Court Square | Hours Restaurant Mon–Thu 11am–11pm, Fri & Sat 11am–midnight, Sun 11am–10pm; Bar Mon–Thu 3pm–2am, Fri 3pm–4am, Sat noon–4am, Sun noon–2am; see website for show times and tickets | Tip The Creek & The Cave isn't the only comedy club in Long Island City. There's also The Standing Room (47-38 Vernon Boulevard, Long Island City, NY 11101, www.standingroomlic.com).

28___Curry Leaves

This is the soup you are looking for

Traveling from New York City to Malaysia to eat a bowl of hawker-style soup would take you the better part of a day. In the world's borough, though, there's no need to hop a flight. Instead, board the 7 train and head to Curry Leaves. You'll have to get up early though. The restaurant's hawker menu is served only from 4am – 11am. The closest thing New York City has to a Southeast Asian night market is this scene where club kids, homesick Malaysians, cabbies, foodies, and the local bookie rub elbows as they wait in line for some of New York's best Malaysian soul food.

The normal menu boasts some 200 items, including classics like Hainanese chicken rice, but from the wee hours until just before lunch, Curry Leaves transforms into a counter set up with a mere half-dozen items, the star of which is a customizable coconut *kari laksa*. Get on line, and when one of the ladies asks what broth and what type of noodles you want, you should specify *kari laksa* with yellow noodles. There are others, but this soul-warming, sinus-clearing combination of springy noodles and rich reddish coconut broth is why you're there. Now comes the fun part – *kari laksa* customization. Choose from several types of fish balls and fish cakes; *char siu* pork; crisp fried wontons; shrimp; Chinese water spinach; and several items stuffed with fish paste, including pillowy blocks of fried tofu, thick rings of bitter melon, and fiery green peppers. Don't be surprised if your bowl winds up being so packed with add-ons you can't see the noodles.

Downtown Flushing's longest running Malaysian pop-up offers other delicacies too. There's *lo mai gai*, a bowl of sticky rice studded with chicken, pork, and mushrooms. And noodles, notably *cheung fen*, springy rice noodles with sweet soy sauce and hot sauce showered in sesame seeds and fried shallots. For dessert grab a *pandan* pudding and an iced coffee.

Address 135-31 40 Road, Suite 1, Flushing, NY 11354, +1 (718) 762-9313 | Getting there 7 train to Flushing–Main Street | Hours Daily 11am–11pm | Tip Continue your exploration of Asian cuisine by sampling one of the many durian delights, including pizza topped with the pungent fruit, at C Fruit Life (135-29 Roosevelt Avenue, Flushing, NY 11354).

29___Cypress Hills Taxidermy
Lions and pythons and bears, oh my

Across from a cemetery is a tableau that looks more like it belongs in the Museum of Natural History than a Queens storefront. Three not so little bears, a towering large brown, and two black bears, stand in one window. The other contains animal skulls and a bobcat. Peer through the glass to see a lion and a deer in mid-leap.

"That bear was in Saks 5th Avenue for the Christmas windows," says John Youngaitis, the owner, curator, and resident taxidermist of Cypress Hills Taxidermy Studio. "And that bear, the medium one, was on Saturday Night Live."

It's not all glitz and glamor for the 63-year-old Youngaitis, who took over the shop and moved it to Queens from Brooklyn shortly after his father died in 2005. Most of his customers are hunters, as can be seen from the many deer heads that line the walls. "The lion and the brown bear I bought from an estate sale," Youngaitis says. "I don't get lions no more," he says, adding that back when his father started in 1958, taxidermists worked with more exotic animals because not so many animals were endangered. Like the big game of taxidermy's past, Youngaitis' craft itself is also endangered; he's the only practicing taxidermist left in New York City.

These days he works mostly with North American animals, including deer, bear, fox, and coyote. There is one exotic he has worked with though. A 20-foot-long reticulated python skin hangs along the back wall. "That was my pet, Axl. It grew to 19 feet and then it died. I wanted it to keep going."

One stuffed bear cub, with its body turned, is uncannily lifelike. Don't be surprised if you feel an urge to pet it. Many curious passersby stop in to take a look and get a photo with the lion or one of the bears, Youngaitis says. "I call it the museum without glass. A zoo you ain't getting that close. A museum they've got glass in front of it, so this is the museum without glass."

Address 71-01 Metropolitan Avenue, Middle Village, NY 11379, +1 (718) 827-7758, www.facebook.com/CHTaxidermyStudio | **Getting there** 7 train to Hunters Point Avenue, Q 67 bus (Middle Village / Fresh Pond Road) at 49th Avenue/21st Street to Metropolitan Avenue/69th Street | **Hours** Mon–Fri 10am–7pm, Sat 10am–4pm | **Tip** After looking at all of Cypress' hunting trophies treat yourself to some hunter's schnitzel, or Jaegerschnitzel as they call the veal cutlets at Zum Stammtisch (69-46 Myrtle Avenue, Glendale, NY 11385, www.zumstammtisch.com).

30_ Donald Trump's First Home

He's just Donny from the block

In 1940, Fred Trump built a five-bedroom Tudor for his growing family in the upscale neighborhood of Jamaica Estates. On June 14, 1946, Donald John Trump was born. Call it a coincidence or not, but the boy born on Flag Day would grow up to become the 45th President of the United States of America.

Donald Trump, or Donny as he was known as a boy, lived in the house with his family until he was four years old when they moved to larger quarters nearby. By his own account, he grew into a rambunctious young man. "I'd throw water balloons, shoot spitballs, and make a ruckus in the schoolyard," he wrote in his 1987 autobiography *The Art of the Deal*. His classmates had a nickname for detention, DTs, so called because young Trump spent so much time there.

"I was always something of a leader in my neighborhood," Trump recalled. "Much the way it is today, people either liked me a lot, or they didn't like me at all."

In the 2016 presidential election, the neighborhood where Trump grew up didn't like him at all, voting overwhelmingly against their native son. Trump took only 13% of the vote. The president's childhood home has proved to be much more popular – at least among real estate speculators – than the man himself.

Five days before Trump was inaugurated, real estate investor Michael Davis sold the property at auction for $2.14 million to Trump Birth House LLC. The individual behind the purchasing company is believed to be a Chinese woman. "This is a house that would otherwise be worth about $1 million dollars, and we sold it for over twice that price," said Misha Haghani, owner of Paramount Realty USA, which handled the auction. It remains to be seen whether or not Trump's first home becomes an official historic site.

Address 89-15 Wareham Place, Jamaica, NY 11432 | Getting there F train to 179th Street, turn right onto Edgerton Boulevard, turn right onto Henley Road, turn left onto Wareham Place | Hours Viewable from the outside only | Tip The house where the future president spent most of his youth is decidedly more palatial. You'll find the stately 23-room brick Georgian Revival on Midland Parkway (85-14 Midland Parkway, Jamaica Estates, NY 11432).

31_Dutch Kills

Go for the cocktails, stay for the ice spears

Before settlers from the Netherlands arrived in 1643, the micro-neighborhood that came to be known as Dutch Kills was called "Canapaukah," or "Bear's Watering Hole," by the Native Americans who lived along the waters that ran through what is now Queensboro Plaza. Today it's home to another kind of watering hole, Dutch Kills, one of the best cocktail bars in New York City.

It's easy to miss the entrance, but for a white sign blinking, "Bar," which guides you like a beacon to the brown door near the corner of Jackson Avenue and Dutch Kills Street. Open it to find a corridor lined with booths decorated with vintage ads for Gilbey's London Dry Gin and Seagram's V.O. Canadian Whiskey.

Make your way to the bar where the backsplashes are painted with the words "Long," "Island," and "City," a tip of the glass to a nearby landmark. Order one of the house classics, like the Game of Death: tequila, grapefruit, lime, sugar, Amaro Meletti, soda, topped off with a dusting of cayenne and smoked sea salt. Or a seasonal drink, like the Tokyo Conference: Japanese whisky, mezcal, banana liqueur, and Amaro Lucano over a rock. Can't find anything you like? The guy or gal behind the bar will gladly make you a bespoke cocktail. "Place your trust in us, for we are more than qualified to satisfy," the menu reads.

You may not give much thought to the ice in your glass, but you can be sure that Richie Boccato, who opened the bar in 2009 with the late Sasha Petraske, has. Before opening Dutch Kills, Boccato tended bar at Petraske's Little Branch, where the bartenders spent hours cutting ice in to different shapes and sizes for drinks. Highball spears, 2-inch cubes, and various size hand-cut rocks enhance the cocktails at Fresh Kills.

"All those implements of torture are used," Boccato says with a nod and a smile toward the ice picks, chisels, hammers, and saws behind the bar.

Address 27-24 Jackson Avenue, Long Island City, NY 11101, +1 (718) 383-2724, www.dutchkillsbar.com | **Getting there** E, M, or R train to Queens Plaza, 7, N, or Q train to Queensboro Plaza, G train to Court Square | **Hours** Sun–Wed 5pm–2am, Thu & Fri 5pm–3am, Sat 5pm–2am | **Tip** Built in the early 1900s, the fountain that graces Court Square Park stands outside what was once the Queens County Court House. Today, the fountain is part of the NYC Parks and Recreation Department's "Fountain Gardens" project, which matches corporate and non-profit donors with opportunities to sponsor park beautification projects (Jackson Avenue between Court Square and Thomson Avenue, www.nycgovparks.org/parks/court-square-park).

32__El Khayam Hookah Bar

Travel to Egypt on a cloud of sweet sheesha smoke

Dozens of hookah bars, many with a distinct nightclub vibe complete with thumping music, line Steinway Street's Little Egypt. One of the very first was El Khayam. In a nod to its pioneer status, the blue awning proudly declares "Godfather of Hookah Lounges, KING OF SHESHA," using the Arabic word for the flavored tobacco that is smoked in bubbling water pipes. With its murals of King Tut, palm trees, and clusters of men playing Egyptian rummy and chess, El Khayam is a veritable oasis of calm amid its more club-like neighbors. Back in 1998 when he opened the lounge named for the Persian poet and scholar Omar Khayyám, Gamal Dewidar let his guests smoke outside on the sidewalk.

"I was driving a taxi, and I felt like every group had their own area – Little Italy, Chinatown – but there was no area for the Arabs," Dewidar recalls. The lounge's other name – Arab Community Center – reflects this vision. Today, many customers hail from Egypt, Morocco, and Lebanon.

The tobacco, pipes, and charcoal are all from Egypt, just like Dewidar himself, who moved to New York City from Cairo almost 40 years ago. Tobacco comes in many different flavors: grape, mint, orange, pineapple, mango, and double apple. "Double apple flavor is the famous one," Dewidar says. Some smokers blend flavors like orange and grape with mint.

Pick your flavor, order your sheesha, and the waiter will bring over one of the dozens of glass pipes, all manufactured by Egypt's famed Khalil Mamoon Hookahs. Foil covers the *hagar*, which contains the tobacco. The waiter will place a few glowing cubes of *fahem*, Egyptian charcoal, atop, and then it's time to partake of one of the most relaxing experiences in Queens. Play cards if you must, but there's nothing like puffing away and enjoying some Egyptian belly dancing videos while drinking sweet mint tea or Turkish coffee.

Address 25-72 Steinway Street, Astoria, NY 11103, +1 (718) 737-4443 | **Getting there** N or Q train to Astoria Boulevard | **Hours** Daily 9am–5am | **Tip** For an Egyptian culinary experience, stop by Ali El Sayed's Kabab Café, where the menu runs to much more than meat on a stick, including such items as whole grilled fish and a marvelous mezze platter (25-12 Steinway Street, Astoria, NY 11103).

33 — Finback Brewery

Glendale's most thirst-quenching secret

With a location tucked away on a residential side street in Glendale, this brewery and tap room are easily overlooked. But if you're a fan of craft beer, you won't want to miss Finback, which has brewed some 150 artisanal beers in its three years of operation and keeps a rotating selection of 8 to 12 on tap.

With sour, dry, hoppy, and lighter beers being poured in the tap room, there's something for everyone says co-founder Basil Lee, who started Finback with head brewer Kevin Stafford in 2014. When Stafford and Lee, who both hail from New England, decided to open in Queens, inspiration struck in the form of a beached whale in Breezy Point, and thus Finback was born, or at least named. Starting out with just the two founders brewing 700 barrels per year, Finback is now on track to produce 5,000 barrels per year. Rather than make the same thing repeatedly in its 25-barrel brewhouse, Finback's philosophy is one of variety. "We enjoy coming up with crazy stuff rather than focusing on one thing and making it over and over again," Lee said.

Double Sess, Finback's take on a wheat beer, definitely falls into the crazy category. The name is a play on words because the beer substitutes Szechuan peppercorn for the more traditional coriander. And then there's BQE, a barrel-aged chocolate coffee imperial stout that pays homage to the Brooklyn Queens Expressway. The strong brew is a collaboration between the two boroughs. Every year Finback uses a coffee from Queens and a chocolate from Brooklyn or vice versa. In the past they've used coffee from Astoria's Native Coffee Roasters and chocolate from Brooklyn's Fine and Raw. "We have a lot of really great support from locals," Lee says. That said, Finback still remains one of Queens' most thirst-quenching secrets. "We still have new customers come in who live not more than three blocks away. People have no idea we are here."

Address 78-01 77th Avenue, Glendale, NY 11385, +1(718) 628-8600, www.finbackbrewery.com | Getting there By car: Long Island Expressway to Exit 19, Woodhaven Boulevard, take Dry Harbor Road and 80th Street to 77th Avenue; by public transportation: 7 train to 69th Street–Fisk Avenue Station then Q47 bus to Glendale, get off at 80th Street and 68th Road | Hours Wed–Fri 5–10pm, Sat 1–10pm, Sun 1–7pm | Tip In Astoria you'll find the Bohemian Hall Beer Garden, which can accommodate 800 thirsty revelers. It was established in the 1900s by the Bohemian Citizens Benevolent Society of Astoria, a group of Czech immigrants, and it even contains a lime tree planted by Vaclav Havel (29-19 24th Avenue, Astoria, NY 11102, www.bohemianhall.com).

34_Flushing Free Synagogue

An opulent historic sanctuary situated in Chinatown

One of New York City's most magnificent synagogues is in an unlikely location: smack in the heart of Chinatown. Steps away, a street cart peddles skewers of Xinjiang-style barbecued meat.

Built in 1926, the Flushing Free Synagogue's entrance stands atop a staircase flanked by bronze menorahs that have taken on a green patina. Four columns support an architrave inscribed: "For mine house shall be called a house of prayer for all people." Above the central double doors is a stained-glass Star of David and in stone the words "Free Synagogue of Flushing." The doorway is crowned by a semicircle engraved with the Tablets of The Law, more commonly known as the Ten Commandments.

A locked gate surrounds it, so you might think the synagogue is closed to the public. But the fence is there to protect it from vandals. It's open for the High Holy Days, and it's also possible to contact the office to schedule a tour.

The sanctuary is topped off by a huge stained glass dome in the pattern of the Star of David, an extravagant blend of Judaica and Georgian neoclassicism. At one time, the dome was so brightly lit that pilots flying into LaGuardia Airport used it as a beacon.

Dazzling stained-glass windows depicting the Twelve Tribes of Israel and Noah's Ark line the walls. Another window features a pair of hands, thumbs touching each other, giving the "priestly blessing," which coincidentally bears a striking resemblance to the Vulcan salute from *Star Trek*. The gesture is performed by Kohanim, or priests, and yes, Leonard Nimoy was inspired by it to create Mr. Spock's signature gesture.

"The synagogue's opulence is representative of the first phase of American synagogues built outside Europe," says Souksavat Soukhaseum, Director of Community Affairs. "You don't see this type of stained glass at other synagogues."

Address 41-60 Kissena Boulevard, Flushing, NY 11355, +1 (718) 961-0030, www.freesynagogueflushing.org | Getting there 7 train to Flushing–Main Street | Hours Office open Mon–Thu 9am–5pm, Fri 9am–2pm; tours by appointment only | Tip Around the corner from the synagogue stands another architectural marvel, the stately Flushing Post Office built in the Colonial Revival style in 1932 (41-65 Main Street, Flushing, NY 11355).

35___Forest Hills Spa

Russian banya as symbolic and literal melting pot

Tucked behind a highway next to the loftily named Calloway Chateau Co-op is a genuine Russkaya banya, or Russian sauna. A clientele as diverse as Queens itself comes to frolic in the pool and sweat it out in the saunas. Peruvian women, young Dominican men, Arab girls in full hijab, and of course, lots of Russians, all come to the spa.

Eucalyptus-scented clouds hang heavily in the steam room, where the temperature hovers at 150°F. Breathe deeply as your pores and lungs open up. At 120°F, the Swedish sauna is slightly less hot. The hottest of all though, is the "Russian Room," which stands at 194°F. Beside a brick oven girded by two black iron bands, a sign cautions: "Be careful! The stones in the saunas are burning hot!"

Within moments of sitting on your towel, you'll start to sweat, or *shvitz*, as one would say in Yiddish. Depending on your tolerance for heat, it might call to mind a medieval torture chamber.

The *platza*, a detoxifying treatment that involves being beaten with bundles of dried oak leaves, approaches torture, but in a good way. It takes place on the uppermost and hottest tier. Lie face down on a moist towel, and cool towels are placed on your head and feet. Then the platza begins, first with a light rustling of leaves and then building in intensity to a good drubbing. Before you sit up, the bundle of blazing hot oak leaves will be pressed into your back. After your chest and shoulders are done, take a quick cold shower and head back for round two. Don't be surprised if you feel dizzy afterwards and need to lie down on one of the benches outside.

"Our grandfathers say you can live up to one hundred years without thinking of diet as long as you do this cleansing banya once a week," says Aleksander Vinar, one of the spa's co-owners, adding that it has benefits for the endocrine system. "We don't sweat enough these days." After a good shvitz session, fortify yourself with some smoked fish and Georgian mineral water.

Address 59-21 Calloway Street, Corona, NY 11368, +1 (718) 699-1919, www.qfspa.com | Getting there E train to Forest Hills – 71st Avenue then Q 23 bus to 108th Street / Horace Harding Expressway | Hours Mon – Thu 3:30 – 11pm, Fri 2 – 11pm, Sat & Sun 9am – 11pm | Tip For a decidedly more modern approach to relaxation, check out Sacred Waters in Long Island City, whose services include a floating tank said to help users attune with their subconscious, reflexology and tribal body art (5-35 51st Avenue, Long Island City, NY 11101, www.sacredwaterslic.com).

36 Forest Hills Stadium

Where kings and queens of music and sports all play

The Beatles, Billie Jean King, Frank Sinatra, Arthur Ashe, The Who, Barbra Streisand. Apart from being household names, they all have one thing in common: all have played at Forest Hills Stadium, a venue that is as fabled in the world of music as it is in the world of tennis.

Before Beatlemania came to Shea Stadium, John, Paul, George, and Ringo landed via helicopter on the grass courts of the West Side Tennis Club for two consecutive sold-out shows in 1964. It began as a haven for tennis players in 1914, and later throughout the 1960s, the music of Frank Sinatra, The Doors, The Rolling Stones, and Jimi Hendrix filled the stadium.

Despite the name, you'll find the West Side Tennis Club and the stadium in the northeastern part of Forest Hills Gardens, situated among majestic English Tudors. The name comes from its original location on Manhattan's West Side. Founded in 1898, the club eventually settled in the then new community of Forest Hills Gardens. Over the years it took on a major role in the world of tennis, hosting the Davis Cup. It was home to the US Open from 1968 to 1978. In the early 1970s, Billie Jean King won there three times. "The game grew from amateur to professional at West Side Tennis Club. It all started there. Most people today would not know that," she said at the time.

And most people wouldn't be able to take in a concert at the classic venue today were it not for the work of local preservationist and historian Michael Perlman. In 2010 the stadium was almost sold and redeveloped into a condominium, but Perlman spearheaded a grassroots campaign that ultimately swayed the club's members to vote against the proposal, paving the way for the redevelopment of one of the most iconic concert venues in New York City.

"I believe the eagles were looking out over Forest Hills and safeguarding the stadium," Perlman says of the stone birds perched atop columns that ring the stadium.

Address 1 Tennis Place, Forest Hills, NY 11375, +1 (718) 268-2300, www.foresthillstennis.com | Getting there E or F train to Forest Hills–71st Avenue | Hours Visit the website for concert schedule | Tip In 1917, Teddy Roosevelt spoke at nearby Station Square to promote the US war effort. Today, the gateway to Forest Hills Gardens is as majestic as ever, with its central plaza and the adjacent Forest Hills Inn, where many acts who played the stadium in the 1960s stayed (20 Continental Avenue, Forest Hills, NY 11375).

37__Forest Park Carousel

Saddle up for a ride on a camel, horse, or tiger

Just inside Forest Park's Woodhaven Gate, you'll find wildlife rarely seen in Queens: a camel, a Bengal tiger, a lion, and dozens of horses all galloping and prancing cheek by jowl. This menagerie is no zoo. It belongs to the Forest Park Carousel, which was built in 1903 by German master woodworker Daniel Carl Muller. It's one of the last two surviving carousels built by D. C. Muller & Bros.

Tally ho as you saddle up on a black horse outfitted with a blue-and-white saddle blanket and a cavalry sword. The horses and beasts in the inner two rings go up and down, while those on the outside stay still. As you spin by, take note of the center ringed by blue panels, each featuring a bearded wizard from whose mouth protrudes a rotating rod that drives the animals up and down. Muller's carvings feature highly realistic anatomy and detailed military regalia like swords and bugles. He studied at the Pennsylvania Academy of Fine Arts, making him one of the few carousel designers with formal training.

There are also mirrors at the center should you be coordinated enough to take a carouselfie without dropping your phone.

Each red spoke radiating from the center terminates in a rectangular panel depicting a scene of days gone by, including 1920s roadsters motoring down Forest Park Drive and 1820s horse races at nearby Union Course.

This is actually the second carousel to spin on this spot. The original Forest Hills Carousel burned to the ground in 1966. In 1972, while searching for a new carousel, concessionaire Restaurant Associates found the 1903 carousel in the possession of Victor Christ-Janer, an architect in Connecticut.

In 2009, the carousel shut down for three years before NY Carousel took over its operations in 2012. A year later it was designated a landmark by the City of New York, making it the only carousel in the city to bear that distinction.

Address Forest Park Drive, Woodhaven, NY 11421, +1 (718) 788-2676, www.forestparkcarousel.com, info@nycarousel.com | **Getting there** R train to Grand Avenue–Newtown, then walk to Broadway and Queens Boulevard and take the Rockaway Park-bound Q53 bus to Woodhaven Boulevard and Myrtle Avenue. Head south on Woodhaven to Forest Park Drive. | **Hours** Daily 11am–7pm | **Tip** After enjoying some old-fashioned amusement, sample a tasty treat at Eddie's Sweet Shop, which has been serving up ice cream sundaes and lime rickeys for more than a century (105-29 Metropolitan Avenue, Forest Hills, NY 11375).

38 Fort Totten Officers' Club

A Queens castle where you can be its king and queen

There's a castle in Queens, but no royalty have ever lived there, although couples do play king and queen when it's rented out for weddings. You'll find the Castle, an impressive structure featuring two octagonal turrets, at Fort Totten, a onetime Civil War army base named for General Joseph Totten, the army's longest serving engineer.

The Castle was designed by General Robert E. Lee and was completed in 1887. The US Army Corps of Engineers, which came to Fort Totten some 20 years prior after leaving West Point, used the magnificent Neogothic edifice as its Officers' Mess Hall and Club. The Corps pulled up stakes after 15 years, although the building, which was originally white, was eventually done up in the Engineers' colors of scarlet and white. That's not the Castle's only tip of the helmet to the Engineers. The design itself, two turrets flanking a central shorter tower, pays tribute to the Corps of Engineers insignia.

The army used the Castle for the next 65 years, and it housed a New York City Job Corps Center from 1970 to 1974. It lay vacant for a decade until the Bayside Historical Society stepped in and restored it in 1986.

The Castle, which is now the home of the Bayside Historical Society, is one of the best preserved buildings on the grounds of Fort Totten. Its neighbor, the Bachelor Officers' Quarters, now lies in a state of decrepitude, unlike the pristine Officers' Club.

In a field not far from the Castle, you'll find what's left of Thorne-Wilkins Cemetery, precisely one gravestone, that of Charles Willets (1781–1833). The one-time cemetery is named for the property's earliest settler, Englishman William Thorne Sr., who established a farm there in 1645.

Fort Totten was built to defend New York Harbor, and the historic stone battery, which offers magnificent views of the harbor and the Throgs Neck Bridge, is also not to be missed.

Address 208 Totten Avenue, Fort Totten, Bayside, NY 11359, www.baysidehistorical.org, info@baysidehistorical.org | Getting there 7 train to Flushing–Main Street then Q16 bus to Fort Totten | Hours The Castle Thu & Fri 10am–4pm, weekends noon–4pm; park hours daily 7am–9pm | Tip You'll find the Lawrence Cemetery at 216th Street and 42nd Avenue. It's part of the original land deed granted by Governor Willem Kieft of New Amsterdam in 1645 to John Lawrence (1618–1699), and the final resting place for multiple generations of Lawrences.

39___Frank Sinatra School of the Arts

Building a legacy through education and art

Across from Kaufman Astoria Studios – a site that's seen the filming of everything from The Marx Brothers' *Animal Crackers* to *Goodfellas*, and *Orange Is the New Black* – stands the Frank Sinatra School of the Arts High School.

Sinatra's pal, Tony Bennett, who grew up in Astoria, founded the school in 2001. It was the brainchild of Bennett and his wife Susan, a social studies teacher, who taught at LaGuardia Community College.

When it opened, the school had one hall and 250 students. Today there are 840 students and five studios devoted to dance, drama, film, fine arts, and instrumental and vocal music. Bennett wanted the school to be part of the community. Its current location opened in 2009, a magnificent glass-walled building that features Sinatra's favorite colors, orange and blue. Principal Donna Finn, says "When you see the glass-faced studio on 35th Avenue, you can look in and see the dancers."

You can also see the students in ticketed public performances at the end of each school year. Each studio holds a show, which have included everything from jazz concerts to Mozart's *Requiem* and musicals like *The Music Man* and *Rent*. Finn says the public really looks forward to the school's shows. "I was at the front desk the other day and someone said, 'What do you have going on?' I said, 'It's summer – school's closed. Come back when we start again in the fall.'"

Bennett still visits, bringing celebrity friends like Billy Joel, Paul McCartney, and Harry Belafonte, all of whom have taught master classes. The crooner has even been known to attend graduation ceremonies. In 2014, he couldn't make commencement, so instead he taught a class on the last day of school and even brought a famous friend, Lady Gaga, with whom he performed several duets.

Address 35-12 35th Avenue, Astoria, NY 11106, +1 (718) 361-9920, www.franksinatraschoolofthearts.org, franksinatrahs@gmail.com | **Getting there** R train to Steinway Street | **Hours** See website for performance schedule and tickets | **Tip** Actor Christopher Walken is another celebrity who grew up in Astoria. The address that once was home to his family bakery, and later the Walken Café, is now a Japanese restaurant, Kondo (29-13 Broadway, Astoria, NY 11106, www.kondorestaurant.com).

40 _ Ganesh Temple

A passage to India via Flushing

Did you know it's possible to travel to India without ever leaving New York City? Spectacular vegetarian food and a Hindu temple make this a destination for both foodie devotees of the crunchy griddled crepes known as dosai and for Hindus who come to worship Ganesh and other devas devas, including Lakshmi and Hanuman.

The spiritual heart of Queens' Hindu community lies a 20-minute walk from downtown Flushing's bustling Chinatown. The ornate Šri Mahā Vallabha Ganapati Devasthānam, the only Hindu temple of its kind in New York City, towers above squat row houses and is visible from a block away.

Consecrated on July 4, 1977, Šri Mahā Vallabha Ganapati Devasthānam, or the Ganesh Temple as it is familiarly known, was the first Hindu temple in North America built with black granite imported from India. Ganesh, the elephant-headed god, is the presiding deva. You'll find him enshrined in a sanctum sanctorum in the temple's center. Ganesh Chaturthi, or Ganesh's birthday, takes place in early September and is one of the most festive times for Hindus in Flushing. The nine-day festival ends with the Grand Ratha Yatrā, a parade where a small statue of Ganesh is led through the streets on a float.

In addition to being a religious center, the temple is also a haven for fans of Indian food. It houses one of New York City's best South Indian vegetarian restaurants, the humbly named Temple Canteen. The cafeteria-style eatery's menu includes more than a dozen types of dosai, crispy ghee-griddled crepes made from a mixture of fermented rice and lentils, including the gigantic crunchy paper dosa.

As for why the Canteen's offerings are so tasty, Dr. Uma Mysorekar, director of the Hindu Temple Society of North America says, "It is a feeling within that you are getting a blessed food instead of running to a restaurant. A restaurant is a restaurant, but a temple is where everybody has good feelings, and that's why things taste so good."

Address 45-57 Bowne Street, Flushing, NY 11355, +1 (718) 460-8484,
www.nyganeshtemple.org, nytemple@gmail.com | Getting there 7 train to Flushing–Main
Street, walk to Main Street and 39th Avenue take Q27 (Jamaica Avenue) bus eight stops to
Holly Avenue and Bowne Street | Hours Mon–Fri 8am–9pm, Sat & Sun 7:30am–9pm |
Tip Continue your exploration of Hindu culture with a visit to the Shri Sirdi Sai Baba
Temple located around the corner at 46-16 Robinson Street (www.dwarakamaishirdi.org).

41 Gantry Plaza State Park

Appreciating the city's rail and industrial past

Almost 100 years ago, the section of the East River that runs along Hunters Point looked vastly different than it does today. It was filled with hundreds of vessels moving freight. Several black transfer bridges, emblazoned with the words "Long Island" in red block letters and visible from the East River, towered above the streets. The black structures still stand – a reminder of the industrial past – and are the namesake feature of Gantry Plaza State Park, which opened in 1998. Technically they are transfer cranes and not gantries, but Transfer Crane Plaza State Park doesn't have the same ring.

The rightmost transfer crane frames the United Nations building, and the piers that extend outward into the East River offer spectacular views of the Manhattan skyline, making this one of the most romantic spots in Queens. If you visit in late May or mid-July, don't miss the park's view of Manhattanhenge, an event in which the setting sun aligns perfectly with the east–west street grid of Manhattan. Not only is it a great place to view Manhattanhenge, Gantry Plaza is also a perfect vantage point for that other breathtaking light show, the Macy's Fourth of July fireworks.

The service dates back to 1925, when a new Long Island Railroad facility was constructed for freight trains. As a car float equipped with railroad track approached the shore, it would be winched tightly to the transfer bridge, where machinery in the black towers raised and lowered the wooden decks of the bridge to the level of the car float. A locomotive would then back onto the bridge and pull the railroad cars into the freight yard.

In the 1960s and 1970s, before they became the focal point for the park, the transfer cranes were a daring if ill-advised rite of passage for teenagers, recalls local restaurateur Gina Cerbone-Teolli, who grew up in the neighborhood. "You had to climb up, go across and go down. All the kids did it."

Address 4-09 47th Road, Long Island City, NY 10007, +1 (718) 786-6385, www.parks.ny.gov/parks/149 | **Getting there** 7 train to Vernon Boulevard–Jackson Avenue | **Hours** Daily 8am–10:30pm | **Tip** Little Bay Park offers East River sunset views of a decidedly less urban nature. Stroll down the jetty to take in a vista that includes Little Bay and the Throgs Neck Bridge (Cross Island Parkway between Utopia Parkway and Totten Avenue, Bayside, NY 11359, www.nycgovparks.org/parks/little-bay-park).

42_ The Geekery HQ

Celebrating geek culture and gaming

Astoria has long been famous for its Greek community and culture. Now Syrus Gabales aims to make it just as famous for geek culture – role-playing games, board games, Star Wars figures, and more – at his shop, The Geekery HQ.

Enter and find yourself in a geek's paradise replete with Simpson's keychains, Kid Robot dolls, and sci-fi and fantasy ephemera. The Geekery also sells dozens of games, from deck builders like Dominion to board games like Vast Crystal Caverns, where players take on the roles of knights, goblins, or dragons. Classics like Clue, Monopoly, and Risk, as well newer ones like Campaign Manager 2008, comprise a board game library. For $5 customers can rent games and play at one of the seven tables. On Wednesday nights, those tables play host to Dungeons and Dragons, the grandaddy of fantasy role-playing games.

"The entire world plays D&D on Wednesday nights," Gabales points out. He opened the shop in 2015 after the group he was playing Warhammer – a miniature fantasy war game – with moved to Brooklyn. "It was too far away to drive every single week," Gabales recalls. "I thought about starting my own group and decided to open a shop."

Although he calls Elmhurst home, Gabales opened in Astoria because he says it has such a strong sense of community. "Astoria's one of the very few places in New York City where people know who their neighbors are," Gabales says.

Warhammer might be his favorite game, but Magic the Gathering – a fantasy trading card game – is by far the store's most popular. A display case contains rare cards, some fetching as much as $400 apiece. Gamers traditionally play Magic on Friday nights, and those who gather at The Geekery HQ are no exception, but the shop also hosts players on Mondays and Thursdays. "We serve the community; the community tells you the games they want to play," he says. "Magic was the one that clicked with Astoria."

Address 42-11 Broadway, Astoria, NY 11103, +1 (718) 606-2853, www.thegeekeryhq.com, hello@thegeekeryhq.com | Getting there M or R train to 46th Street | Hours Mon–Fri 2–11pm, Sat 11am–11pm, Sun 11am–8pm | Tip If all that gaming has made you hungry, check out Gabales' favorite soup spot, Shuya Café de Ramen (42-13 Broadway, Astoria, NY 11103).

43__Golden Shopping Mall
The O.G. Flushing Chinatown food court

If downtown Flushing is arguably America's best Chinatown, then the ramshackle Golden Shopping Mall and Food Court is surely one of its best hawker centers. Open the door to this subterranean food court and you'll be greeted by all sorts of delicious aromas. The bottom of the stairs brings you to Sichuan by way of Cheng Du Tian Fu where Chinese food expert Fuchsia Dunlop exclaimed, "It's just like being in China!"

Favorites include cold noodles slicked with chili oil, garlic, and mouth-tingling Sichuan peppercorn and *fu qi fei pian*, a cool tangle of offal – beef tongue, tripe, and tendon – with a romantic back story. The couple who invented it had such a harmonious union that their specialty was dubbed *fu qi fei pian*, or husband and wife offal slices. It sings with signature Sichuan *ma la* – or numb hot flavor – a combination of warming chilies and fiery Sichuan peppercorn. Chili-drenched curds of snow white *ma po tofu* and water-poached fish swimming in a fiery sauce are also excellent.

In the center is Tian Jin Dumpling House. What started out as a humble purveyor of Northern Chinese-style *jiaozi* now offers 10 types of steamed dumplings. The best are the subtle sea bass scented with ginger and green onion and lamb and green squash, which emit a puff of pleasantly lamby vapor when bitten into. Customize your dumpling sauce by mixing chili paste, black vinegar, soy, and garlic.

Just past Tianjin on your left is Xi'an Famous Foods, which specializes in food from Western China, including flatbread lamb sandwiches seasoned with cumin and green hot peppers and fresh hand-pulled *biang biang* noodles with cumin lamb. Cold skin noodles, or *liang pi*, consist of blocks of squidgy wheat gluten and slippery starch noodles in a sauce of garlic, chili, vinegar, and, in a nod to the region's Silk Road influences, tahini. It is one of the best cold noodle dishes in New York City.

刀削麺
SLICED NOODLE

燒烤
B B Q

- WONTON PULLED NOODLE
13. ROAST DUCK PULLED NOODLE
14. STEWED PULLED NOODLE
- OX TRIPE PULLED NOODLE
- BEEF INTESTINE PULLED NOODLE
- PORK INTESTINE PULLED NOODLE
18. TUBE BONE PULLED NOODLE
19. PORK MEATSAUCE PULLED NOODLE
20. CALM PULLED NOODLE
21. HOUSE SPECIAL HANDPULLEDNOODLE
22. HOUSE COLD HAND PULLED NOODLE

混沌拉面（刀削面）$5.50
烤鸭拉面（刀削面）$7.50
猪骨拉面（刀削面）$6.00
牛百叶拉面（刀削面）$6.00
牛肚拉面（刀削面）$7.00
大肠拉面（刀削面）$6.00
筒骨拉面（刀削面）$5.00
炸酱拉面（刀削面）$5.00
海瓜子拉面（刀削面）$6.00
兰州楼拉面（刀削面）$7.50
兰州凉面（刀削面）$4.00

1. SQUID STICK
2. BEEF STICK
3. LAMB STICK
4. CHICKEN STICK
5. CHICKEN WING STICK
6. CHICKEN LEG STICK
7. FISH BALL STICK
8. MUSHROOM STICK
9. TOFU STICK
10. CHICKEN HEART STICK
11. VEGETABLE STICK

拉面（刀削面）$9.50
大拉面（刀削面）$5.00
猪拉面（刀削面）$5.50

No Smoking

寿司 SUSHI

正宗蘭州拉面

Address 41-28 Main Street, Flushing, NY 11355 | **Getting there** 7 train to Flushing–Main Street | **Hours** Daily 10am–9:30pm | **Tip** Take a tea break at the nearby Fang Gourmet Tea, where a flight of some excellent cha will set you back a mere $5 a person (135-25 Roosevelt Avenue, Flushing, NY 11354, www.fangtea.com).

44__Gottscheer Hall

A century of German hospitality in Ridgewood

Set amid a tree-lined block christened Gottscheer Avenue, a German watering hole harkens back to a simpler time. That time was 1924 when the white building with the blue awnings touting banquets and weddings first opened its doors.

Once inside, you'll be greeted by German beauty queens, and lots of them. Framed photos of young women wearing blue sashes that read "Miss Gottschee" line the entrance. The crowning of Miss Gottschee has been going since the hall was founded almost 100 years ago by immigrants from Gottschee, which was once part of Austria-Hungary and now lies within Slovenia. Ask any German of a certain age who grew up in Queens though, and chances are they have fond memories of parties held in the banquet room. Such parties, like the annual Cozy Corner Fishing Club Spring Dinner Dance, which features the Heimat Klange Orchestra, still take place.

An old map of Gottschee is framed on a wall across from the L-shaped bar next to a lighted panel sign that reads "Hat Check." These days the young nighttime patrons bellying up to the bar to hoist dimpled glass steins of Spaten and tall tapered glasses of Franziskaner Weissbier are more likely to be sporting baseball caps than fedoras. Rock music prevails on the jukebox, playing AC/DC, The Who, and Neil Diamond. There are also classics of a decidedly Germanic nature. A CD by The Adlers Band with such songs as "Auerhan Yodeler" sits above Fleetwood Mac, and Die Schlauberger's "Play it Loud" shares the same page as Guns N' Roses.

The kitchen offers bratwurst and krainerwurst with a choice of sauerkraut or potato salad. If you're feeling especially hungry, get the platter with both sausages and both sides. As befits a German beer hall, there are pretzels, small and large. The latter is as big as your face and should provide ample fuel for an evening of drinking and chatting with your neighbors.

Address 657 Fairview Avenue, Ridgewood, NY 11385, +1 (718) 366-3030,
www.gottscheerhall.com | Getting there M train to Forest Avenue | Hours Tue–Thu & Sun
1pm–midnight, Fri & Sat 1pm–3am | Tip Continue your exploration of Gottschee culture
and cuisine with a visit to Morscher's Pork Store, which specializes in German and Eastern
European sausages and cold cuts (58-44 Catalpa Avenue, Ridgewood, NY 11385,
www.morschersporkstore.com).

45__Gurdwara Sahib

Sikhism and a brush with Hollywood fame

Around the corner from the Punjabi Diner and Singh Farm, a gold dome glitters above rows of two-story homes. It belongs to the Gurdwara Sahib of the Sikh Cultural Society. *Gurdwara*, as Sikh temples are known, translates to "guru's door." It was opened in 2011 after the first one was destroyed by a fire, according to Harpreet Singh Toor, a community organizer who was chairman of the Sikh Cultural Society at the time. Toor hired architect Amarjit Singh Sidhu who pored over Sikh history books to inspire his creation.

"They are not looking at just bricks and walls, they are looking at a building which has historical significance," Toor says of people who come to worship.

Once inside, remove your shoes and socks. Take an orange kerchief to cover your head and enter the gurdwara. The building and the room where people worship share the same name.

A pink canopy topped with a broad brass arch hangs over the altar. It's crowned the *ik onkar*, a symbol that denotes that there is one god. Behind the altar is the *khanda*. It consists of two curved swords surrounding a circle at whose center is a double-edged sword. The circle signifies the universal nature of humanity, and the double-edged sword signifies the impartiality of god's justice. Go downstairs afterwards to the *langar* and enjoy a free vegetarian meal with chants of "Wa guru" in the background.

If you're a movie buff, the gurdwara might look familiar. It was featured in the 2014 film *Learning to Drive*, which tells the story of a Manhattan writer and her Sikh driving instructor. Before Sarah Kernochan began her script, she consulted with Toor, who showed her what life was like for Sikhs living in Richmond Hill. Toor went on to coach Sir Ben Kingsley on how to act like a Sikh and even has a small part as a priest. "They had my picture on the wall as a priest and I was like, you must be joking," Toor recalls.

Address 95-30 118th Street, South Richmond Hill, NY 11419, +1 (718) 846-3333 | **Getting there** F train to Union Turnpike – Kew Gardens then Q 10 bus to Lefferts Boulevard / Atlantic Avenue | **Hours** Open for prayer daily from 4am – 9pm, langar is open at all times | **Tip** After visiting the temple that was featured in a Hollywood production, take in a Bollywood movie at Bombay Theatre (68-25 Fresh Meadow Lane, Fresh Meadows, NY 11365, www.bombaytheatre.com).

46 Harry Houdini's Grave

The master magician never to escape again

Without Harry Houdini there would be no David Copperfield, Penn & Teller, or David Blaine. The legendary escape artist and magician was buried in Glendale 90 years ago, but his grave in Machpelah Cemetery continues to be a destination for fellow magicians.

Machpelah is part of a mile-long stretch of Jewish cemeteries that run along Cypress Hills Street. Houdini, born Ehrich Weiss, established the plot where more than a dozen of his family, including his mother and father, are buried. You can see the plot from the cemetery gates. At the back, up three steps, is the master magician himself: a bust of Houdini sits atop a pedestal engraved with the names Houdini and Weiss. Just below is a beautiful red and gold mosaic design bearing the crest of The Society of American Magicians, which Houdini presided over from 1917 until he died on Halloween in 1926. The bust is unusual because graven images are typically forbidden in Jewish cemeteries. Nevertheless, it was placed there in 1927. Over the years, it has been vandalized and stolen. Finally in 2011, the Scranton, Pennsylvania-based Houdini Museum placed a new one there.

Houdini's not buried in the rotunda though. His grave is on the left side of the plot. The flat granite marker reads "Houdini 1874–1926," and it's covered with stones according to Jewish tradition. You'll also see items more magical in nature: keys left by escape artists, coins left by prestidigitators, and of course playing cards.

On Halloween in 1926, The Society of American Magicians held the first-ever broken wand ceremony at the grave wherein a magician's wand is broken denoting that after death the wand has lost its magical powers. The ceremony was held on Halloween for years, but it started attracting too many revelers and was moved to November. But you don't have to wait until then to pay your respects to the father of American magic.

Address 82-30 Cypress Hills Street, Ridgewood, NY 11385, +1 (718) 366-5959 | Getting there J train to Cypress Hills then a 20-minute walk along Cypress Hills Street | Hours Sun–Fri 9am–4pm, closed on Jewish and national holidays | Tip Roger "Rogue" Quan, an Elmhurst-based professional magician, counts himself a disciple of Houdini. Catch his show at The Lobster House at 8pm, Mon–Thu (95-25 Queens Boulevard, Rego Park, NY 11374, www.seafoodbucketexpress.com/free-magic-show).

47 Hell Gate Bridge

The Bermuda Triangle of Queens

Earlier this year, Hell Gate Bridge, which connects rail traffic between Wards Island and Queens, celebrated its 100th anniversary. The bridge, whose tower and curved span soar above Astoria looms large in popular culture and local ghost stories. It's been featured in the films *Serpico* and *Queens Logic*.

Walking the ghost track, an unused track without a rail bed, was a rite of passage for local teens, says Mitch Waxman, a local tour guide and publisher of the website Newtown Pentacle. "If you see the ghost train coming for you, you've got to get out of the way, or it's going to sweep you to hell," he says. Another urban myth said there was a child molester who lived in a chamber in the tower that was covered with pictures of his victims.

Lore about the turbulent strait for which the bridge was named predates its construction by more than a century. Dutch explorer Adriaen Block dubbed the dangerous waters Hellegat, or in English Hells Gate. In 1780, the HMS *Hussar*, a Royal Navy frigate laden with $5 million of gold, sank to the bottom.

By the late 1800s, the swirling waters had claimed so many lives that New York City turned to the US Army Corps of Engineers to render the waters navigable. In 1885, the Corps set off what was then the largest manmade explosion in an attempt to alter the underwater geography. The blast was heard as far away as Princeton, NJ. Despite these efforts to make it safe, tragedy struck once again at Hell Gate in 1904 when the *General Slocum* caught fire, killing more than 1,000 people.

Hell Gate Bridge even played a role in World War II when the Nazis' failed Operation Pastorius landed German agents on American soil in 1942 in hopes of wrecking the bridge. "Hell Gate looms large in American history," Waxman says. Of course, the park also makes a great place for a picnic, unless you're scared of ghosts of drowned sailors.

Address Shore Boulevard and Ditmars Boulevard, Astoria, NY 11105 | Getting there
N train to Ditmars Boulevard Station then walk northwest on Ditmars Boulevard | Hours
Unrestricted | Tip High on a hilltop overlooking Long Island Sound is Steinway Mansion,
a granite and bluestone edifice originally constructed in 1858 by Benjamin Pike, Jr., a
manufacturer of scientific instruments. Look closely for the cut-glass windows that depict
Pike's handiwork (18–33 41st Street, Astoria, NY 11105, www.steinwaymansion.org).

48__HiFi Records and Café

Deep grooves, local tunes, and strong java

The first thing you'll notice about HiFi Records and Café, the only shop in Queens that combines vintage vinyl and espresso, are all the records in the window. The Clash, Devo, Nirvana, N.W.A., and Forest Hills' native sons The Ramones are all on display. Take a closer look though, and you'll see that each album cover features kittens instead of band members.

The whimsical window display is an indicator that although Javi Velazquez, the shop's owner, is serious about vinyl and turntables, he doesn't take himself too seriously.

"It's kind of like HiFi without the stress or the attitude," Velazquez says of his shop, which carries high-end Rega Research turntables and stocks thousands of records from rockers and pop-rockers like Nick Cave and King Crimson, to punk acts like the Buzzcocks and the New York Dolls. There's even a section devoted to bands from Queens: Sick Walt, The Gantry, and Better Head.

HiFi Records also holds concerts in the small shop. "We move the bins out of the way," Velazquez says. The store basically became a music hub when it opened two years ago. "If you're a musician, do you want to play in a restaurant where you're not really engaging the crowd because everybody's trying to eat? No. Here you have a captive audience because people that come here are driven by music."

Velazquez himself is driven by music, having worked in record stores as an adolescent. He inherited a substantial collection of folk and rock records from his sisters when their tastes shifted toward disco. "I've been a record lover and a music lover all my life," says Velazquez, who amassed a collection of 25,000 LPs before opening the shop.

Ask him who his favorite Queens' musicians are, and he'll immediately say, The Ramones, and then quickly namecheck some other biggies. "Simon and Garfunkel, Louis Armstrong, Tony Bennett, all of them have made an impact."

Address 23-19 Steinway Street, Astoria, NY 11105, +1 (718) 606-1474, www.hifi-records.com, whatsup@hifirecords.com | **Getting there** N or W train to Ditmars Boulevard | **Hours** Mon–Thu noon–7pm, Fri & Sat noon–8pm, Sun noon–6pm | **Tip** Located in a former soap factory, local watering hole Joe's Garage is just down the street from the auto body shop where the owner worked for more than 30 years. It features live music as well as brews from Astoria craft brewer SingleCut Beersmiths (45-01 23rd Avenue, Queens, NY 11105, www.facebook.com/JoesGarageAstoria).

49 Himalaya Connection
The world's rooftop in a basement emporium

Handicrafts, cooking equipment and ingredients, religious statues, snacks, and many other products from the rooftop of the world can be found in this subterranean shop in the heart of Jackson Heights' Himalayan community.

When Himalaya Connection's owner Dawa Sherpa came to America in 1997, there weren't many Nepalese living in Queens. In 2001 there was a major influx from the Himalayan diaspora, and in 2006 he opened the shop, which specializes in products from Nepal, Tibet, Bhutan, and India.

Brass buddhas line the shelves along with prayer wheels and offering bowls. The Tibetan buddhist tapestries known as *thangka* hang from the walls. Packages of incense, including Tibetan Potala brand – named for that country's Potala Palace – sit above bags of Sichuan peppercorn. Known as *timur* in Nepalese, the tiny dried seeds produce a tingling sensation on the palate.

"Nepalese and Tibetans mix the peppercorns with pickle. It tastes really good," Sherpa says. Other pickles, including pouches of pickled buffalo meat flavored with chili and cumin, line the shelves.

One of the fieriest of all is Druk Dalla Chili made from round berrylike *dalle khursani* peppers. "It's a really spicy one – our people love it spicy," Sherpa says with a laugh.

Other ingredients include momo masala for seasoning the filling of the beef dumplings that are as popular in Jackson Heights as they are in Nepal, Tibet, and Bhutan. The store even sells the steamers used to make them.

Nepali soccer jerseys share a rack with the colorful hats known as dhaka topi . At the back, find a tableau that sums it all up: an ornate image of the elephant-headed Indian god Ganesh sits beside a photo of the Potala Palace with the Dalai Lama superimposed. Above his head are a rainbow and a dove holding the Tibetan flag.

Address 72-30 Broadway, Jackson Heights, NY 11372, +1 (718) 505-9200, www.himalayaconnection.com, himalayaconnection@gmail.com | Getting there 7, E, F, M, or R train to Jackson Heights–Roosevelt Avenue | Hours Daily 9am–midnight | Tip Get some *momo* on the go from the A&G Himalayan Fresh Food cart located just around the corner at 73rd Street and Roosevelt Avenue.

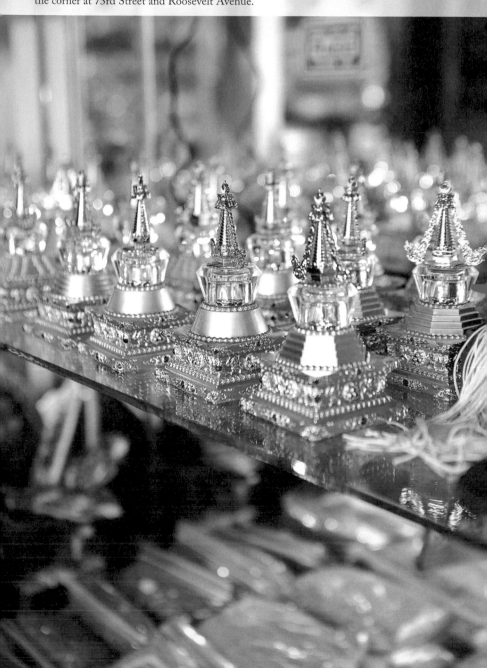

50_Jackson Heights Historic District

European-influenced foyers, gardens, and griffins

The neighborhood of Jackson Heights was originally envisioned as an alternative to Park Avenue in Manhattan. The buildings borrow from a variety of European architectural schools, from the sparse English Edwardian to the elaborate Spanish Romanesque. The Jackson Heights Historic District is the birthplace of the garden apartment – complexes built around interior gardens – and the first cooperative apartment building in America.

George H. Wells built the first apartment building, Laurel Court, on 82nd Street at Northern Boulevard, not far from a trolley to Manhattan. In 1917, the elevated subway opened along Roosevelt Avenue and paved the way for more development by Edward A. MacDougall's Queensboro Corp., which could now boast that its burgeoning community was only 20 minutes from Grand Central.

Andrew J. Thomas designed the most striking buildings, including The Chateau (34-05 to 34-47 80th Street), which was built in 1923, with slate mansard roofs and two winged griffins that face each other above the entrances inspired by French architecture. MacDougall liked The Chateau so much he moved his family from Flushing to a sumptuous 14-room duplex there with sweeping views of New York City from the Battery in Manhattan to Hell Gate in Queens.

Across the street from The Chateau is The Towers (33-15 to 33-51 80th Street), which Thomas built in 1924 and features marble hallways, oak parquet floors, and gardens. The griffin motif from The Chateau appears once more on The Towers in the form of two large statues guarding the gardens.

MacDougall's original vision for Jackson Heights was to model it after a concrete bungalow community that Thomas Edison had built in New Jersey. It's a good thing that he changed his mind.

Address Bounded by 76th–88th Streets and Roosevelt Avenue–Northern Boulevard, Jackson Heights, NY 11372 | **Getting there** 7 train to 82nd Street–Jackson Heights | **Hours** Unrestricted from outside only | **Tip** One of Queens' most picturesque planned communities – Forest Hills Gardens – designed by Grosvenor Atterbury and patterned after England's garden cities, lies just a 20-minute subway ride away. Begin your exploration at Station Square's Forest Hills Inn and head south along Continental Avenue (20 Continental Avenue, Forest Hills, NY 11375).

51__Jam Master Jay Memorial
Pay your respects to Run-D.M.C.'s Big Beat Blaster

Before they cut their first album, rap pioneers Run-D.M.C. rocked the mic at Hollis Park, nicknamed Two-Fifths Park. Joseph Simmons, later known as Run, and Darryl McDaniels, later known as D.M.C., rapped over beats and cuts created by DJ Jason Mizell, later known as Jam Master Jay.

"He's Jam Master Jay the big beat blaster," Run-D.M.C. sang on Live at Hollis Park. "JMJ are the letters of his name. Cuttin' and scratchin' are the aspects of his game." The group forever changed hip-hop style with their black leather coats, heavy gold chains, fedoras, and laceless Adidas Superstar sneakers, which were immortalized in the 1986 hit, "My Adidas." The love letter to the trio's favorite footwear led to a million dollar endorsement deal. In 2011, for the song's 25th anniversary, a sneaker emblazoned with the year 1986 and the monogram JMJ across the back was released as a tribute to Jam Master Jay, who was murdered in his recording studio in 2002.

You'll find a mural dedicated to his memory diagonally across the street from Two-Fifths Park. "The Best DJ in the US of A," is written in a combination of block letters and script. A portrait of Jay sits in the center above two turntables and a pair of Adidas. It was painted shortly after his murder.

In 2009, the corner of 250th Street and Hollis Avenue was renamed Run-DMC JMJ Way. A second copy of the green street sign sits in the window of In The Chair Barber Shop (202-13 Hollis Avenue). Look closely and you can see traces of the signatures of scores of people who signed it.

"Everybody's on there, all the OGs from Hollis," says the shop's owner Debra Hammond, who grew up with Jam Master Jay, Run, and D.M.C. Among the now faded famous names are DJ Hurricane of the Beastie Boys, D.M.C., Run, and Russell Simmons. "Everybody came through and signed this. I cherish it.

Address 250th Street and Hollis Avenue, Hollis, NY 11412 | **Getting there** F train to Parsons Boulevard, walk to 153rd Street and Hillside Avenue then catch Q83 bus to Murdock Avenue and 202nd Street | **Hours** Unrestricted | **Tip** A few blocks away on 200th Street, you'll find a mural devoted to Queens' rap legends, A Tribe Called Quest. It also pays tribute to Marcus Garvey, Richard Wright, Ralph Ellison, and Maya Angelou.

52 Jamaica Bay Wildlife Refuge

An urban oasis for humans and birds alike

Peering north past rustling marsh reeds that gird the 45-acre West Pond, Manhattan's glittering World Trade Center Tower One seems a world away. Yet the Jamaica Bay Wildlife Refuge, the only wildlife refuge in the entire United States National Park System, is only an hour from downtown Manhattan.

The 120-acre East Pond and 45-acre West Pond serve as beacons to migratory birds, from rarely seen black-necked stilts to more common Canada geese. Pick up a Birds of Jamaica Bay Checklist, which features more than 325 species, from the Visitor Center.

Birds aren't the only wildlife that wing their way toward the salt marshes and upland fields, Monarch butterflies are among 70 species that appear in late summer and early fall. There are hundreds of wildflowers as well, from white blossomed field chamomile and yellow cypress spurge in spring to pink sand spurry and green clotbur in late summer. A hike of the West Pond Trail behind the Visitor Center is a great introduction. Be sure to look for the osprey platform. If you're lucky you might even spy one of the fish-eating hawks as it plunges feet first into the bay to capture a fish with its strong talons.

On the way back to the Visitor Center, record anything you've seen on your hike in the Bird Log. Don't be surprised if you see such entries as, "Muskrat with three young," as the refuge is home to plenty of other fauna besides birds, including one of the largest horseshoe crab populations in the Northeast.

Even if you don't manage to get up close and personal with any wildlife, you'll have gotten a respite from New York City's hustle and bustle. And West Pond is only the beginning: there are five miles of trails in total to explore, including Big John's Pond, a quarter-acre habitat for reptiles and amphibians.

Address 175-10 Cross Bay Boulevard, Broad Channel, NY 11693, +1 (718) 318-4340, www.nyharborparks.org/visit/jaba.html | Getting there 7 train to 61st Street–Woodside Station then take Q53 Rockaway Park bus | Hours Trails daily from sunrise to sunset; Visitor Center daily 9am–5pm | Tip Some of the best pizza in Queens can be found nearby at New Park Pizza (156-71 Cross Bay Boulevard, Howard Beach, NY 11414, www.newparkpizza.com).

53 Jamaica Performing Arts Center

The light of dance and music shines brightly

An imposing brick-clad building with two towers rests on the corner of 153rd Street and Jamaica Avenue, home to the Jamaica Performing Arts Center (JPAC), a 400-seat theater that is host to jazz, dance, and theater performances.

As a plaque between the arched entranceways notes, the site dates back to 1715 when a church was built there, rebuilt in 1833, destroyed by a fire in 1857, and rebuilt again in 1858. "This edifice is dedicated to the worship of the triune god in 1859," reads the plaque over the one-time house of worship that has become a temple of the performing arts.

The First Reformed Dutch Church was built in the early Romanesque revival style and designed by master carpenter Sidney Young with the assistance of master mason Anders Peterson. Former Governor Mario Cuomo served as an altar boy here in the 1940s.

Above the pair of arched doorways are three magnificent stained-glass windows that bathe the front area in light. The central window features Jesus with outstretched arms flanked by angels. In front of it is a coiled DNA light sculpture hanging from the ceiling, suggesting that a propensity for both worship of the divine and enjoyment of the performing arts is intrinsic in human nature.

The stained-glass windows are not original to the church. In the early 1970s, the diocese closed the church, and for decades the land-marked skeleton of the building sat in disrepair, its central campanile visible from passing Long Island Railroad trains.

In 2008, thanks to a $22-million redevelopment effort spearheaded by the Greater Jamaica Development Corp., the building was restored to its former grandeur. JPAC was awarded the Lucy G. Moses Award, the New York Landmarks Conservancy's highest honor.

Address 153-10 Jamaica Avenue, Jamaica, NY 11432, +1 (718) 618-6170, www.jamaicapac.org, jpac@jcal.org | Getting there E train to Jamaica–Parsons/Archer | Hours Mon–Fri 10am–5:30pm, see website for performance schedule and tickets | Tip The Jamaica Center for Arts and Learning (JCAL), JPAC's parent organization, is housed inside another nearby historic building, the neo-Renaissance Queens Register of Titles and Deeds Building. Today, it features art studios, galleries, and a theater (161-04 Jamaica Avenue, Jamaica, NY 11432, www.jcal.org).

54_Kalpana Chawla Way

Commemorating a South Asian space hero

Look up at the corner of 74th Street and 37th Road and you'll see a sign that reads "Kalpana Chawla Way." It's named for the first Indian-American astronaut, who was a hero to many people in India, all over South Asia, and the diaspora.

In 2004, the block of 74th Street between 37th Road and 37th Avenue was renamed to honor Chawla, who died along with six other astronauts in the space shuttle Columbia disaster on February 1, 2003.

"The thing that's most impressive is when people walk by this block and they see the sign some will know and some won't know who she was," New York City Mayor Michael Bloomberg said at the time of the street's dedication. "They'll stop, hopefully, and look and say that must have been somebody that made a difference."

On November 19, 1997, Chawla became the first Indian-born woman in space. "We are proud of you. Each one of us in India is proud of you," then Indian Prime Minister I. K. Gujral told Chawla as she orbited the Earth.

Not only was Chawla a pioneer in space, she was the first woman to ever enroll in the aeronautical engineering course at Punjab Engineering College in Chandigarh. J. R. D. Tata, who flew the first mail flights in India, inspired her to take up flying.

Nearby Butala Emporium (see ch. 17) sells Indian comic books that tell the legends of gods and real-life heroes like Gandhi, and yes, Kalpana Chawla, whose beaming visage shines on the cover.

Despite the fact that she was a pioneer and inspiration to many in India and elsewhere, the modest Chawla never saw herself that way. "I never truly thought of being the first or second someone," she told India Today after her first space flight. "This is just something I wanted to do. It was very important for me to enjoy it. If you want to do something, what does it matter where you are ranked? Nor does being a woman make a difference. We were all just crew members."

Address 74th Street between 37th Road and 37th Avenue, Jackson Heights, NY 11372 | **Getting there** 7, E, F, M, or R train to Jackson Heights–Roosevelt Avenue | **Hours** Unrestricted | **Tip** Did you know that Jackson Heights is home to a penguin? Well, actually it's a bronze statue of a penguin that's been nicknamed Wink. Local resident Elcy Carballo dresses up the 2-foot-high statue in costumes for various holidays, including Christmas, Easter, and Colombian Independence Day (Elmjack Mall, 75th Street and 37th Road).

55__King Manor Museum

18th-century espionage at the home of a founding father

The home of Rufus King, one of America's founding fathers, is in the heart of Jamaica. King purchased the house in 1805 with every intention of retiring from politics after an illustrious career that included fighting in the American Revolution, helping frame the US Constitution, and serving as a US senator and US ambassador to England. The passing of his friend and ally Alexander Hamilton left King as one of the last Federalists and spurred him to get back into the Senate and diplomacy, serving into his 70s.

King was one of the youngest members of the 1787 Constitutional Convention. A wrought-iron fence adorned with the Preamble to the United States Constitution surrounds King Manor to commemorate his participation.

King Manor functioned as a working farm and a laboratory for agricultural experimentation, as well as a source of commercial profit. King wrote and received hundreds of letters discussing the state of his crops and agricultural practices.

Today, King Manor is a museum and features many artifacts, including a Jamaica stage letter box from the early 19th century that was used to send written communications. Elsewhere in the museum's collection, you'll find a box that was used to send the 18th-century equivalent of top secret transmissions, a leatherbound diplomatic dispatch kit that King used when he was ambassador to England. Correspondence would be placed inside, and the box would be locked and shuttled back and forth across the Pond.

"It was a very secure method of correspondence," says Kelsey Brow, King Manor Museum's curator. "It was like using a locked briefcase or a secure email server today for diplomatic communications." Likely topics of the messages include brokering trade between the US and England, as well as arranging for the Marquis de Lafayette, who fought in the Revolutionary War, to be freed from an Austrian prison.

Address 150-03 Jamaica Avenue, Jamaica, NY 11432, +1 (718) 206-0545, www.kingmanor.org, contact@kingmanor.org | **Getting there** E train to Sutphin Boulevard–Archer Avenue, F train to Parson Boulevard | **Hours** Mon–Fri noon–2pm, Sat & Sun 1–5pm | **Tip** Continue your exploration of neighborhood history with a visit to Grace Episcopal Church, which was founded in 1702 and features a graveyard with tombstones dating from the early 1700s and bearing the names of early Jamaica's Dutch and English settlers (155-03 Jamaica Avenue, Jamaica, NY 11432, www.episcopalchurch.org/parish/grace-episcopal-church-jamaica-ny).

56 Kissena Park Velodrome

Feed the need for speed

If you're a cyclist feeling the need for speed, or if you just want to witness some old-time traditional track racing, there's only one place in New York City to go: the Kissena Park Velodrome.

The pitched curves and steep embankments make it possible to achieve speeds of 30 and even 40 miles per hour. Every Wednesday evening from the end of April to the end of August, Alan Atwood, president of Atwood Racing Services, hosts the Twilight Series on the "track of dreams." Atwood says that what makes the Kissena Park Velodrome unique is the 400-meter length, which is twice that of some newer courses.

Typically there are 15 races with varying formats, including scratch races, which are run for a set number of laps with the top five taken at the finish, and chariot races, where a holder pushes the rider at the start of the one-lap race. The latter is a favorite of Amir Toussi who was born and raised in Flushing and works at Deluxe Cycles in Brooklyn. "I like how simple it is: one really hard effort," he says. "You've got a guy holding you at the start who pushes you as hard as he can, and you take it from there."

The clanging of a town-crier-like bell signals the end of each race. Many racers are youngsters from ages 9 to 14, who have been taught how to ride fixed gear track bikes by the NY Parks Department's StarTrack program. Unlike conventional bikes, those used for track racing have no brakes and only one gear.

The velodrome was built in 1964 by Robert Moses for the Olympic Trials, when the track's cyclists dominated, taking five of eight places on the US squad. Over the years, the track fell into disrepair and was once such a rough ride that it earned the nickname "Big Bumpy." In 2004 Mayor Michael Bloomberg spent $500,000 to refurbish the Velodrome. Whether you're riding or watching a race, there's nothing like being part of the action at the track.

Address Booth Memorial Avenue and Parsons Boulevard, Flushing, NY 11355,
www.kissenavelodrome.info | Getting there 7 train to Flushing – Main Street, Q17 bus to
Kissena Boulevard / Rose Avenue | Hours Daily dawn – 9pm | Tip The Velodrome is located
inside Kissena Park, where you will also find Kissena Lake. Encircled by weeping willows,
the lake makes a perfect spot for a picnic or afternoon stroll (164th Street and Lithonia
Avenue, Flushing, NY 11355, www.nycgovparks.org/parks/kissena-park).

57_Kitty Genovese Murder

A grisly murder and a social phenomenon

When the Mowbray building in Kew Gardens was built in 1926, it was the height of luxury, with a roof garden and iceless refrigerators. It was also the neighborhood's tallest building.

However, the Mowbray has a far more macabre claim to fame. In the wee hours of March 13, 1964, some 38 witnesses were said to have watched from their windows as Kitty Genovese, a 28-year-old bartender returning from work, was brutally stabbed to death by Winston Moseley, a psychopathic serial killer.

Two weeks later, *The New York Times* published an in-depth article about the murder, "For more than half an hour 38 respectable, law-abiding citizens in Queens watched a killer stalk and stab a woman in three separate attacks in Kew Gardens."

At around 3am, Genovese noticed Moseley at the end of the LIRR parking lot and headed up Austin Street toward Lefferts Boulevard, where there was a police call box. Moseley overtook her near what is now Austin's Alehouse, stabbing her twice with a hunting knife and causing her to scream, "Oh, my God, he stabbed me! Please help me!"

Lights went on in the Mowbray, and a man's voice cried out, "Let that girl alone!" Moseley walked off for a few minutes before returning to find Genovese struggling in the entrance to her building, where he stabbed her several more times.

For years afterwards, the witnesses' behavior during the murder was cited as both an example of urban apathy and bystander syndrome. Years later, in its obituary of Moseley, the *Times* reported that several neighbors did in fact call the police.

"Yeah, there was a murder," said local historian Joseph De May in a *Times* piece published for the slaying's 40th anniversary. "Yeah, people heard something. You can question how a few people behaved. But this wasn't 38 people watching a woman be slaughtered for 35 minutes and saying, 'Oh, I don't want to be involved.'"

Address 82-62 Austin Street, Kew Gardens, NY 11415 | **Getting there** E or F train to Union Turnpike–Kew Gardens Station | **Hours** Unrestricted from outside only | **Tip** Nearby in the picturesque Station Square of Forest Hills lies the site of another horrific murder. In the winter of 1977, David "Son of Sam" Berkowitz shot and killed Christine Freund while she sat in a car with her date. Slugs recovered from the scene helped police to conclude that they were dealing with a serial killer (20 Continental Avenue, Forest Hills, NY 11375).

58 The Knockdown Center

The threshold of culture in a former Maspeth door factory

Located on a stretch better known for warehouses than arts centers sits one of Queens' up-and-coming art institutions, the Knockdown Center. The name refers to the 50,000-square-foot former factory's previous life as the headquarters of Manhattan Door, where Samuel Sklar invented the Knock-Down door frame in 1956, so named because it could be shipped in pieces or "knocked down."

The factory closed in 2011, and the Knockdown Center opened in 2013 thanks to a family member who wanted to transform it into a center for the arts. The vast central room features exposed beams, brick walls, and plenty of light. It holds 1,800 people and has hosted everything from an evening of Indonesian music to the rapper Young M.A. The center also features more intimate performance spaces and art galleries.

"Some know us as an art museum, but other people know us as a concert venue," says Tara Plath, Knockdown's communications and marketing director. "There was one night when we had a metal show in this space, a dance party in this space, and a queer POC rap show in the small space in the back," Plath recalls. "All those people were in the bar. That's when we're happiest."

The bar, known as The Ready Room, pays homage to Knockdown's industrial past with reclaimed wood and lighting repurposed from work stations. One wall proudly displays the original Manhattan Door Factory sign, while a table holds multicolored shards of glass from the space's days as the Gleason-Tiebout Glass Company. When the building was being renovated a small hill of glass was found outside. It turns out that it was right below a window, and whenever the manager wasn't around workers threw their mistakes out the window.

Outside the factory you'll find The Ruins, which are the shells of brick buildings, where a summer music series called Overtime is held. Look for the beehives on the roofs.

Address 52-19 Flushing Avenue, Maspeth, NY 11378, +1 (347) 915-5615, www.knockdown.center, mail@knockdowncenter.com | Getting there L train to Jefferson Street, B 57 Maspeth bus to Flushing Avenue/54th Street | Hours Exhibitions: Thu & Fri 5–9pm, Sat & Sun 2–8pm; Bar: Thu & Fri 5pm–midnight, Sat 2pm–2am, Sun 2pm–midnight; for concerts and special events please see website | Tip Maspeth has long had a Lithuanian population, a fact reflected in the architecture of the Church of the Transfiguration, which was designed by a Lithuanian architect and features a steeple that resembles a Lithuanian roadside shrine (64-14 Clinton Avenue, Flushing, NY 11378, www.ststanstrans.org).

59 __ LaGuardia Landing Lights

Watching jumbo jets roar just overhead

This oddly named New York City park, really a series of nine lots that lay along a flight path to LaGuardia Airport, was created in 1958 when the Port Authority surrendered the land to New York City for recreational purposes. Their placement is mandated by Federal Aviation Administration regulations, which require a swath of clear land in approaches leading up to runways.

The lights themselves, pole-mounted spotlights surrounded by fences complete with stern warnings not to tamper with them, aren't particularly impressive. The real show takes place when Runway 4 is in use, typically on overcast days when the wind is coming from the north. At other times, the only things you'll likely see flying around are dragonflies and pigeons.

A great place for you to start your plane-spotting adventure is the large parcel on the corner of 79th Street and 25th Avenue. When the conditions are right, it's possible to observe dozens of jumbo jets from various carriers – Delta, United, American, and more – roaring by overhead. It's absolutely breathtaking the first time one goes by overhead, and it remains pretty magnificent even after the first half-dozen sightings. Young men and children play soccer seemingly oblivious to the planes, which appear to be scarcely higher than the treetops.

To insure that you get a view, you'll want to check the day's wind conditions. Again, you're looking for the wind to be coming from the north. It's also well worth downloading a mobile application called Plane Finder. Check it and you can even see if planes are using the diagonal approach which cuts right through 79th Street and 25th Avenue.

For an even closer look, head to 24th Avenue and 81st Street, where the jets dip lower as they approach Runway 4 while taxi drivers hang out and ignore the show going on right above their heads.

Address 79th Street and 25th Avenue, Elmhurst, NY 11370, www.nycgovparks.org/parks/laguardia-landing-lights | Getting there E, M, R, or 7 train to Roosevelt Avenue–Jackson Heights then Q 47 bus to 25th Avenue and 79th Street | Hours Accessible 24 hours | Tip Hardcore plane spotters can be found at Planeview Park, which offers what some might consider disconcertingly close views of the jets, a mere 30 yards overhead (Ditmars Boulevard between 82nd and 87th Streets, East Elmhurst, NY 11369, www.nycgovparks.org/parks/planeview-park).

60_Latimer House Museum
The Flushing man who brought light to the masses

If you're reading this page by electric light, or if you have ever used a telephone, an African American inventor, electrical pioneer, and the son of fugitive slaves named Lewis H. Latimer played a role. It's a fact that you won't find in many history books, but thankfully his legacy has been preserved in the house in Flushing where he lived from 1903 until his death in 1928.

When Latimer bought the Queen Anne-style residence in 1902, Flushing was predominantly white. At the time, he was one of only 200 African Americans in the greater New York area to own a home. Even though he helped develop both the electric light and the telephone, the house lacked both when he moved into it.

After fighting in the Civil War, Latimer went to work in 1865 as an office boy for patent law firm Crosby Halstead and Gould. Soon he became interested in drafting. By 1872, he was the firm's head draftsman. While there he helped Alexander Graham Bell with the patent for the telephone, enabling Bell to beat competitor Elisha Gray.

Latimer invented the carbon filament light bulb in 1879 while working for the U.S. Electric Lighting Co. Latimer's longer lasting cheaper filament ultimately paved the way for the widespread development of electric lighting. While he was with U.S. Electric, Latimer supervised the installation of the first electric lighting in New York City at the Equitable Building.

Latimer went to work for the Edison Electric Light Co. in 1884 as a draftsman and an expert witness in patent litigation on electric lights. In 1890, he wrote a book explaining the new technology to the general public, most of whom did not have electric lighting at home.

"Like the light of the sun, it beautifies all things on which it shines, and is no less welcome in the palace than in the humblest home," Latimer wrote in 1890, 13 years before he came to call Flushing home. Quite a poetic description for technological innovation.

Address 34-41 137th Street, Flushing, NY 11354, +1 (718) 961-8585, www.latimernow.org | **Getting there** 7 train to Flushing–Main Street, walk to Northern Boulevard and turn left, make a left onto Leavitt Street, which will be the third block on the left | **Hours** Wed, Fri & Sun noon–5pm | **Tip** In the center of Northern Boulevard, a majestic winged woman sculpted out of Georgia pink marble stands sentinel to commemorate lives lost in World War I. Flanked by two benches, she was sculpted by Hermon Atkins MacNeil and dedicated in 1925 (Northern Boulevard and Leavitt Street, Flushing, NY 11354).

61__Lhasa Fast Food

Culinary enlightenment in the back of a cell phone store

Tucked between a purveyor of Indian bridal jewelry and a sari shop lies a passage to culinary nirvana. You might be thrown off by the orange sign that reads "Prabhu Money Transfer" or the cell phone stores flanking either side of the corridor. You'll know you're in the right place when you spot Lokeshwor, the 11-headed, 3,000-armed bodhisattva. Look up and you'll see Tibetan prayer flags criss-crossing the ceiling. Press on to find yourself in Lhasa Fast Food, Jackson Heights' secret Tibetan restaurant.

Above the counter is a tribute to Tibet. The Dalai Lama beams, framed in a golden khata scarf, against Mount Kailash, a peak revered by both Buddhists and Hindus. On the left next to a Tibetan flag is a sign that reads "shide," or peace in Tibetan. The whole thing sits on a gold roof below which reads "Lhasa Fsat Food."

There's nothing fast about the food here though. Rather than a Tibetan Burger King, Sang Jien Ben's five-year-old restaurant is really a home away from home for immigrants from the Himalayan diaspora. *Momo*, the juicy pleated beef dumplings seasoned with Sichuan peppercorn, celery, ginger, and garlic are the most popular item. Almost every table holds a bamboo steamer filled with the dumplings, which are as popular in Jackson Heights as they are in Tibet. Lhasa Fast Food's dumplings are award winning. In 2014, they took top honors in the Momo Crawl, an annual event where hundreds come to the neighborhood. The trophy, a golden momo atop a mountain sits on the counter. Try the *chu-tse momo*, a variety that adds green chives to the mix. Other items on the menu include *thenthuk*, a soup whose noodles take the form of irregular swatches of chewy dough, and *laphing sherpo*, a yellow mung bean noodle aggressively seasoned with garlic and roasted chili. Ben even makes a sushi version where the yellow strands wrap around a chunk of gluten. He got the idea from working at a sushi place.

Address 37-50 74th Street, Jackson Heights, NY 11372, +1 (646) 256-3805 | **Getting there** E, F, M, or R train to 74th Street–Jackson Heights | **Hours** Daily 11:30am–10:30pm | **Tip** After your Tibetan repast, sit for a spell in the aptly named Diversity Plaza (37th Road between 73rd and 74th Streets). Keep an eye out for seasonal and cultural events.

62 LIC Flea & Food

International eats and antiques with a skyline view

Colombia, Jamaica, Japan, Mexico, and Peru are just a few of the nations that are represented at LIC Flea & Food. You'll find the outdoor food/flea market in Long Island City alongside the East River. It's especially apt that this international market offers stunning views of the United Nations.

Grab a brisket sandwich from Butcher Bar, an American barbecue outfit that smokes its meat overnight, or a savory Japanese pancake from Oconomi. Both businesses are run by Astoria natives. Wash it all down with some suds from one of Queens' many microbreweries.

LIC Flea founder and owner Josh Schneps counts Oconomi among his favorite vendors and points out that his vision was to create an international food market. The original name when it opened in 2012 was LIC Flea and International Food Bazaar. When the market first opened, the flags of every nation represented were flying next to the adjacent Plaxall warehouse. It was in the warehouse where Schneps found the giant cable spools that would become the market's tables. "They had the industrial charm. We sanded them down, laminated them, and put our logos on them," he said.

Schneps grew up going to the flea market at Aqueduct Racetrack, which, until it closed in 2010, was the largest outdoor flea market in Queens. That experience, a love for the LIC's views of the Manhattan skyline, and the diversity of cuisines in Queens inspired him to open the market. Many of the same furniture and antique vendors have been with LIC Flea & Food from the very beginning. These days they're joined by Colombian handicrafts from Proveeartes and T-shirts inspired by historic Queens documents from Dutch Kills Klotheing. The market has even been featured on HGTV's Flea Market Flip.

Whether you're in the mood for Peruvian from Don Ceviche or Italian from Giuseppe Piadineria or Southeast Asian from I Eat Lao, LIC Flea & Food has got you covered.

Address 5–25 46th Avenue, Long Island City, NY 11101, +1 (718) 224-5863, www.licflea.com | **Getting there** 7 train to Vernon Boulevard–Jackson Avenue | **Hours** Sat & Sun 11am–6pm, spring through fall | **Tip** Explore multiple aspects of Irish culture, including Gaelic lessons, fiddle playing, and Irish set dancing, at the New York Irish Center (10-40 Jackson Avenue, Long Island City, NY 11101, www.newyorkirishcenter.org).

63__Local Project

An LIC art gallery with neighborhood roots

Carolina Peñafiel has been in Queens since long before it became cool, i.e. when Lonely Planet named it the No. 1 US destination for 2015. Peñafiel is one of the founders of Local Project, a Long Island City art gallery that also runs mentoring programs and art residencies.

Peñafiel established Local Project, whose logo is a vinyl record with the letters LP, in 2003. "We realized there was a need for a space not only to hang out but to present work or do creative things," the Chilean-born photographer says. Today, you'll find Local Project on 44th Road, and depending on the exhibit, you'll see everything from Latin American photography to the works of Issa Ibrahim, a painter whose work draws on classic comic books and hails from Jamaica, Queens. There are block parties on weekends, and every summer there's a garage sale featuring artists' supplies, records, and books.

Recently, Peñafiel began selling works from Chilean artists beside the shop's signature T-shirts, which feature a spray paint can writing in graffiti script above the words, "Queens is not new, established 1637."

The T-shirt is both a nod to Local Project's former location in the now demolished graffiti mecca 5Pointz and Peñafiel's roots in the neighborhood.

"There was a whole time where everyone said, 'You've gotta come to Queens,'" Peñafiel recalls. "We've been here forever; it's always been cool to us. We've always loved it." When she and her friends overheard someone utter the phrase, "Queens is not new," they decided to turn it into a T-shirt.

"We've been lucky to be able to stay in the neighborhood," says Peñafiel, who at one time had considered moving Local Project to Harlem. Fortunately her landlord offered her space in a building that had once housed a massive marijuana growing operation that was busted in 2013. "Sometimes you get the ghost of the weed smell."

Address 11-27 44th Road, Long Island City, NY 11101, +1 (646) 298-0969, www.localproject.org, info@localproject.org | **Getting there** E, M, G, or 7 train to Court Square | **Hours** Tue – Sat noon – 6pm | **Tip** SculptureCenter showcases works by emerging, established and international artists in what was once a trolley repair shop (44-19 Purves Street, Long Island City, NY 11101, www.sculpture-center.org).

64 Locals Surf School

Learn the break in a Queens' beach town

Ever wanted to learn how to hang ten? There's no better place in Queens than Locals Surf School. A web search shows the address as 66-17 Seaspray Avenue, but the school's just off the boardwalk on Beach 69th Street. On most days, that's where you'll find its founders, Mike Kololyan and Mike Reinhardt, amid the crashing waves and sea spray. The two have been surfing in the area for 20 years and know the break really well, which is an important aspect of teaching. "You go anywhere, you want to learn from the locals," says Kololyan.

The first thing you'll learn before even touching a surfboard is how to wriggle into a form-fitting wetsuit. Should you opt to take a class in the winter – surf school's in session all year – the gear includes a hood and gloves. "The waves are good and the crowds real light in the winter," Reinhardt says.

Whether you're taking a group or individual class, the next lesson is basic surfboard anatomy: nose, tail, and rails. Don't expect a sleek wooden or fiberglass number. Instead you'll be given 9-foot blue soft-top learning board. A pro board is "great for speed and maneuverability, but not so great when it goes up in the air and lands on your head."

Before getting in the water, you'll be shown two crucial moves: the prone paddle and the popup. As the name suggests, the latter involves quickly rising to a riding stance on the board.

Once in the water, the teacher will guide you to the takeoff zone and show you how to ride a wave. Reinhardt says that a common mistake rookie riders make is looking at their feet, which is a good way to tip over. "It's like learning to walk on a tightrope. You don't really stare at your feet, you pick a point in the distance and use your mind's eye to balance."

Sometimes it takes a whole lesson before a student can get on their feet, but most are able to ride at least one wave within their first lesson.

Address Beach 69th Street and the Boardwalk, +1 (347) 752-2728, www.localssurfschool.com, info@localssurfschool.com | **Getting there** A train to Beach 67th Street | **Hours** Lessons daily from 9am–3:30pm, bookable through website | **Tip** "I don't make sand castles. These are more like mashups of brutalist architecture," says sand artist Calvin Seibert, who like the two Mikes, can be found at Beach 69th Street most every day of the year.

65 Louis Armstrong House

Pops' home for listening and viewing pleasure

New Orleans-born jazz trumpeter and American cultural icon Louis "Satchmo" Armstrong will forever be associated with his hometown whose airport bears his name. But Corona, Queens, is also a large part of his legacy, thanks to an unassuming two-story brick house located on 107 Street, a short walk from the 7 train.

The house was constructed by Thomas Daly in 1910. The Brennans, an Irish American family, called it home until 1943, when Armstrong and his wife purchased it. Newlyweds, Satchmo and Lucille could have settled anywhere in the world, but they chose Queens. Armstrong lived and worked in the house until he passed away on July 6, 1971, two days after the date that he claimed to be his birthday. Armstrong believed he was born on July 4, 1900 but in the mid-1980s, Armstrong expert Tad Jones discovered a baptismal certificate that shows Satchmo was born on August 4, 1901. The museum celebrates the jazz legend's birthday on both dates.

Since 2003 the Louis Armstrong House has functioned as a museum and offers guided tours. Nobody has lived there since the Armstrongs; thus it offers a window into Satchmo's style – from a sleek custom kitchen done up in all-blue enameled cabinetry to a bathroom featuring a gold swan faucet fixture. Jazz aficionados will be particularly keen to see the library's reel-to-reel tape recorders. The tour also features audio clips and visitors can hear Pops practicing his trumpet, enjoying a meal, or talking with friends.

As can be seen in numerous archival photos, Satchmo often hung out with local youth and taught them to play music. The museum continues this tradition of community involvement with several concerts and events throughout the year, including a summertime Jazzmobile block party. The house is shown only through guided 40-minute tours that start every hour on the hour (last tour of the day starts at 4pm).

Address 34-56 107th Street, Corona, NY 11368, +1 (718) 478-8274, www.louisarmstronghouse.org | Getting there 7 train to 103rd Street–Corona Plaza. Walk north on 104th Street. Turn right onto 37th Avenue then turn left onto 107th Street. The Louis Armstrong House is on the left, turn right onto 37th Avenue. | Hours Tue–Fri 10am–5pm, Sat & Sun noon–5pm; always open on the 4th of July, in honor of Armstrong's traditional birthday | Tip Treat your fellow jazz fans to Corona's finest Italian pastries and cappuccino at the nearby Mama's Backyard Café (46-10 104th Street, Corona, NY 11368).

66_Mae West's Grave

Come up to Cypress Hill Abbey and see her sometime

Before there was Madonna, and before there was Marilyn Monroe, there was a brassy Brooklyn-born blonde named Mary Jane "Mae" West who blazed the path for female sex symbols in Hollywood. You've probably heard many of her infamous one-liners, including "Is that a gun in your pocket or are you just glad to see me?" which was actually uttered during her last film, *Sextette* (1978).

What you might not know is that the bawdy star is buried in Queens at Cypress Hills Cemetery. It's ironic that the star was laid to rest at Cypress Hills Abbey. After all, she made her name by playing a character who was far from being a nun.

To get to Mae West's final resting place, you'll have to start in Brooklyn and travel to Queens, much like she did. West was born in Bushwick, but her family moved to Woodhaven where legend has it she first performed in public at Neir's Tavern (see ch. 71). It's only fitting that she's interred in a cemetery that straddles both boroughs.

Make sure to stop by the cemetery office and tell them you're going to visit Mae West's grave. For one thing they'll need to have somebody unlock the facility, and for another you'll need a map to help you make the 30-minute trek to Queens. Don't worry – the friendly lady at the counter will plot a route for you. On the way to Queens, you'll pass hundreds of graves, including that of Dr. Thomas Holmes, who introduced the practice of embalming during the Civil War, and a plot devoted to Chinese Americans.

Once you've crossed under the Jackie Robinson Parkway and entered Queens, you're only a short walk away from Cypress Hills Abbey. You'll find West on the second floor in Section EE. The West family area is decorated by a bouquet of artificial pink, white, and yellow roses and features handwritten notes from adoring fans, including "John from Lower Manhattan" who had just watched *I'm No Angel*, before paying his respects to the legendary sex symbol.

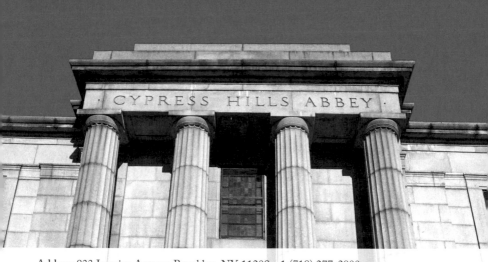

Address 833 Jamaica Avenue, Brooklyn, NY 11208, +1 (718) 277-2900, www.cypresshillscemetery.org | **Getting there** J train to Cypress Hills Station then walk to Abbey, get map at cemetery office | **Hours** Daily 8am – 4:30pm | **Tip** Barbra Streisand is still very much alive, but that didn't stop the star of stage, screen, and song from building an ornate Art Deco mausoleum for herself and her family. You'll find it at Mount Hebron Cemetery in section 104 near the road (130-04 Horace Harding Expressway, Flushing, NY 11367, www.mounthebroncemetery.com).

67 __ Malcolm X's Queens Home
Civil rights history in the shadow of LaGuardia

With boulevards named for Frederick Douglass and Malcolm X, Harlem is steeped in civil rights history. But did you know that Queens has a claim to fame? Even though he's usually associated with Harlem, Malcolm X called Queens, specifically East Elmhurst, home from 1959 until he was assassinated in 1965.

Apart from a stretch of 97th Street that was renamed Malcolm X Place in 2005, there's no indication that Malcolm lived there with his wife Betty Shabaaz and their four daughters.

Just off the corner, you'll find a key lime pie-colored house where they lived. It was the only house on the block when it was built in 1924. In the 1960s, the Nation of Islam purchased the house and gave it to Malcolm X and his family. Before that, they had been living nearby at 25-26 99th Street. Many other prominent African Americans, including Harry Belafonte and Willie Mays, also called the neighborhood home. In 1964, shortly after Cassius Clay, later named Muhammad Ali, defeated Sonny Liston in Miami, Malcolm X showed the boxer houses near his own in an effort to get him to move to Queens.

The iconic photo of Malcolm X holding an M1 carbine rifle as he peers outside the venetian blinds was taken inside what was then a modest brick home and appeared in the September 1964 issue of *Ebony* magazine as part of an article called the "Mystery of Malcolm X." It was no prop. After his break with the Nation of Islam, Malcolm X grew concerned about death threats.

On Valentine's Day 1965, he was sleeping next to his wife when he was startled awake by a series of explosions and a screech of tires at 3am. He quickly gathered up his family and led them out of the house, which had been set ablaze by three Molotov cocktails.

"It doesn't frighten me," Malcolm X said in response to the bombing before leaving to give a talk in Detroit. "It doesn't quieten me down in any way or shut me up."

Address 23-11 97th Street, East Elmhurst, NY 11369, www.queenslibrary.org/research/special-collections/black-heritage-reference-center-of-queens-county | Getting there N train to Astoria–Ditmars Boulevard, walk to Hoyt Avenue and 31st Street then catch M60-SBS bus and get off at 94th Street and 23rd Avenue | Hours Unrestricted, accessible from outside only | Tip You'll find the Black Heritage Reference Center of Queens County at the Langston Hughes Library in Corona, a neighborhood where jazz greats Cannonball Adderly and Dizzy Gillespie once lived (100-01 Northern Boulevard, Corona, NY 11368, www.libraryactioncommittee.org/langston-hughes-community-library/history).

68_Marine Air Terminal

An Art Deco masterpiece from the golden age of air travel

"You can travel like a real mensch," Queens Borough Historian Dr. Jack Eichenbaum says of LaGuardia Airport's remarkably well-preserved Marine Air Terminal, where Delta operates shuttle flights to Chicago. Terminal A offers a glimpse of 1940s air travel. It was built in 1939 to accommodate the gigantic Boeing B-314 seaplanes known as flying boats. You don't have to actually fly anywhere though to check out the Art Deco masterpiece.

Little has changed since it was designed by Delano and Aldrich. Bas relief flying fish – a tribute to the flying boats – circle the two-story building. Once inside you'll find yourself in a rotunda dominated by a 235-foot-long circular mural called *Flight*. Painted by Abstract Expressionist James Brooks, it chronicles man's conquest of the skies, from ancient times when the mythical Icarus flew too close to the sun to Da Vinci's flying machines to the modern era as represented by the Wright Brother's historic flight. It concludes with a flying boat, a Pan American Clipper.

A replica of *Yankee Clipper* hangs beneath a skylight. It was one of 12 flying boats that flew out of the terminal from 1940 to 1945. Eleanor Roosevelt christened the *Yankee Clipper* on March 3, 1939. On March 31, 1940 more than 100,000 people came to what was then known as LaGuardia Field to witness the takeoff of the plane as it embarked on the first transatlantic flight to Lisbon.

"The real purpose of aviation is to bring the peoples of the world closer together," said New York City Mayor Fiorello La Guardia in his remarks to the crowd. A bust of the mayor who gave the airport its name sits in the center of the rotunda.

Be sure to check out the entranceway to The Yankee Clipper restaurant, which functions as a de facto museum of sorts with numerous black-and-white photos, including one of Franklin Delano Roosevelt enjoying a slice of birthday cake aboard a flying boat.

Address 5 Marine Terminal Road, www.laguardiaairport.com/news/la-guardias-art-deco-marine-air-terminal | **Getting there** 7 train to 69th Street then Q47 bus to LaGuardia Airport Terminal A | **Hours** Open 24 hours daily | **Tip** Treat yourself with a Manhattan worthy of Don Draper at Mar's (34-21 34th Avenue, Astoria, NY 11106, +1 (718) 685-2480, www.lifeatmars.com).

69_Mohan's Tattoo Inn

A temple of ink via Kathmandu

Smiling Tibetan masks and fierce Buddhist protector gods adorn the walls. A carved wooden temple dog guards a black leather couch and Buddha sits serenely in the corner. You might think that it's a shrine, but it's not. It's a temple to the fine art of tattooing, Mohan's Tattoo Inn.

Master tattoo artist Mohan Gurung hails from Kathmandu, Nepal and opened the shop in 2015. Gurung, who has been practicing his craft for 22 years, had opened a Kathmandu shop in 2000. He used to travel to the States to attend tattoo conventions. A 2007 visit to Jackson Heights, where he experienced the robust Nepali community firsthand, inspired him to open Mohan's.

"I saw there was no Nepalese tattoo shop," Gurung recalled. "Everybody said I should open one. Finally in 2014 I came here and started working on it." About half of his customers are Nepali. His work is rich in cultural references, from a portrait of a Sherpa smoking a pipe and the Himalayas themselves to a hand wrapped around a prayer bell and the Dalai Lama. Other imagery includes Hindu gods and Buddhist mantras. Gurung says that mandalas, the geometric patterns used in Buddhist practice, are a trend these days. He also has Mexican clientele and once even created a skeletal Virgin of Guadalupe for a client. Small tattoos run to about $60. Larger pieces are priced at a rate of $120 per hour.

"I'm scared of doctors' needles," says Gurung, whose entire body is a canvas of tattoos. "The nurses laugh at me and ask why am I scared of needles. The doctor's needle goes really deep you know; I feel really uncomfortable. The tattoo needle only goes through the upper layer of the skin."

Gurung has never done a Queens-themed tattoo, unless you count momos, the dumplings beloved in both Nepal and Tibet. As part of the annual Momo Crawl, a yearly festival organized by Jeff Orlick, he gives tattoos of the crimped dumplings for free.

Address 77-02 Roosevelt Avenue, Jackson Heights, NY 11372, +1 (718) 898-1700, www.mohanstattooinn.com, mohantattooinn@gmail.com | **Getting there** E, F, M, or R train to 74th Street–Jackson Heights | **Hours** Mon–Fri noon–10pm, Sat & Sun noon–9pm | **Tip** Can't commit to getting a tattoo? Why not get *mehndi*, or Indian henna art, along your hands and forearms at Hanu Beauty Salon? (81-46 Baxter Avenue, Elmhurst, NY 11373, +1 (347) 891-7798)

70__Muncan Food Corp.

A family business steeped in smoke and tradition

The first thing you notice at this Romanian charcuterie shop is the aroma. An intoxicating blend of spices and cured pork pervades the air. The second is dozens of sausages and spare ribs hanging above the counter. The next thing would be Latino countermen speaking Romanian, Hungarian, or Serbo-Croatian.

"We always call it the United Nations," Marko Stefanovic, owner of the shop, says of the staff's affinity for foreign languages. It stems from a desire to connect with customers. "Some of them speak better Romanian than I do, and I grew up with it."

The third-generation charcuterie shop owner also grew up with the cured and smoked meats that crowd the deli cases. "My father used to take me to the shop on Saturdays. If he didn't take me, I'd start crying."

Back in 1978 when Stefanovic's grandfather, Tima Muncan, set up shop, the neighborhood was primarily Greek and Italian. When it started, Muncan Food Corp. was 90% butcher and 10% charcuterie. That 10% comprised Romanian products like *domeca*, a paprika-flavored dried sausage that Stefanovic says is his favorite for snacking.

Cvarci, Romanian pork cracklings made from chunks of pig jowl are another of his favorites. "When that's hot and you have hot bread with it, I don't think there's a better bite," he says.

These days the shop is 90% charcuterie and 10% butcher. This is largely due to Miodrag "Mike" Stefanovic, Marko's father, who came to America in 1983. People would bring samples of dried sausages to the master charcutier and ask if he could replicate them. "My Dad would say, 'Yeah it's ok, but I'll make you something even better,'" Stefanovic recalls.

Today, Muncan sells 200 varieties, including such non-traditional items as lamb prosciutto and duck prosciutto. "You're not going to find those in Eastern Europe," Stefanovic says. "That was really my father – he's always experimenting."

Address 43-09 Broadway, Astoria, NY 11103, +1 (718) 278-8847; 60-86 Myrtle Avenue, Ridgewood, NY 11385, +1 (718) 417-5095; www.muncanfoodcorp.com | **Getting there** Astoria location M or R train to 46th Street; Ridgewood, M train to Fresh Pond Road Station | **Hours** Mon–Fri 8am–6:30pm, Sat 8am–6pm | **Tip** After shopping for some artisanal charcuterie sip some artisanal tea at Tea & Milk, who first got their start at LIC Flea & Food (see ch. 62) (32-02 34th Avenue, Astoria, NY 11106, +1 (347) 921-2056, www.teaandmilk.com).

71 Neir's Tavern

Serving up Woodhaven community spirit since 1829

Belly up to the very same bar that once played host to Mae West, Goodfellas, and W. C. Fields. Cross the threshold to find yourself in a tavern steeped in history. It all started with an 1820s racetrack. At the time Union Course was the most famous track in the US, pitting thoroughbreds from the South against ones from the North. "The Race of the Century" drew 100,000 spectators in 1823. The racecourse's popularity spurred the manager, Cadwallader R. Colden, to open the Blue Pump Room in 1829.

Louis Neir bought the bar in 1898 and changed the name to Neir's Social Hall, adding a bowling alley, ballroom, and catering. The Neir family owned the tavern up until 1967. Some of the bar's older patrons remember working as pinboys, earning the princely sum of a nickel a game to reset the lanes.

Today, Colden's bar goes by the name Neir's and retains the original mahogany bar and ice-chilled beer system. When Loycent Gordon took over in 2009, it was renamed Union Course Tavern. Many still referred to it as Neir's after the family who owned it longest. "Instead of naming it after myself I wanted to honor the family that had it way before me so I returned it back to Neir's Tavern," Gordon says.

The bowling alley and ballroom are long gone, but Neir's retains its historic identity. Legend has it that Mae West made her debut there. A portrait of the saucy actress dolled up in a shimmering gown and feather boa graces one wall. Other famous patrons are said to have included real estate mogul Fred Trump, father of US President Donald J. Trump. Were it not for Gordon, Neir's would not be around today. "The landlord was getting a lease signed with a bodega to occupy the space," Gordon says. "There's a delicate balance between development and preserving history. I believe Neir's Tavern and a lot of the things Queens has to offer are part of the fabric of New York City history," Gordon says.

Address 87-48 78th Street, Woodhaven, NY 11421, +1 (718) 296-0600, www.neirstavern.com |
Getting there J train to 75th Street–Elderts Lane Station | Hours Mon–Thu 11am–1am,
Fri & Sat 11–2am, Sun noon–1am | Tip Not far from Neir's find an address that sex symbol
Mae West once called home: 89-05 88th Street, Jamaica, NY 11421.

72 Noguchi's Garden and Ashes

A garden as sculpture and gallery

On the far reaches of Long Island City, you'll find the only Japanese garden in Queens. In addition to katsura, pines, and a bamboo grove, the garden at the Noguchi Museum features American trees like magnolia and birch. It's really a Japanese American garden, which reflects the artist's Japanese American heritage.

Like many Japanese gardens, there are water elements, notably Isamu Noguchi's take on a *tsukubai*, a traditional basin used to purify oneself before entering a temple. Called *The Well*, the basalt piece is the opposite of a *tsukubai*. Instead of being dipped into, the water flows outward, offering a reflection of the katsura tree's rustling leaves.

"The garden as a whole is a sculpture, and then there are individual pieces," says Shannon Murphy, the museum's head of education. They include the towering two-tone granite *Helix of The Endless*, which Noguchi finished in 1985, three years before his death. Half of his ashes were scattered in a corner by a small granite sculpture, Uruguay. The rest of the ashes were scattered by his studio in Mure, Japan.

Before Noguchi established the museum in 1985, the garden was little more than a junkyard. He had been living and working in Queens since 1961. His move to Long Island City was partly motivated by the proximity of marble and stoneworks. Look out the window of Area 9 and 10, and you can see his original studio at 33rd Avenue and 10th Street.

Experience what it's like to be a sculptor with one of the museum's Hands-on at Noguchi classes, which include stone carving. Students work with five-pound blocks of alabaster.

We're not right by the subway. You have to mean to come," says Jennifer Lorch, the museum's deputy director. "I would think he's happy people are making the pilgrimage and coming with purpose."

Address 9-01 33rd Road, Long Island City, NY 11106, +1 (718) 204-7088, www.noguchi.org, info@noguchi.org | **Getting there** R train to 46th Street then Q104 bus to Vernon Boulevard and 33rd Road | **Hours** Wed–Fri 10am–5pm, Sat & Sun 11am–6pm | **Tip** The ramshackle Dream Park features some really crisp wild-style graffiti and a few sculptures (Broadway and Vernon Boulevard, Long Island City, NY 11106).

73_ Ohel Chabad-Lubavitch
Thousands seek inspiration at the Rebbe's grave

When he was alive, Rabbi Menachem M. Schneerson, the revered Chabad Lubavitch Rebbe, who is considered to be the most influential rabbi in modern history, would visit the grave of his father-in-law, the sixth Lubavitcher Rebbe, Rabbi Yosef I. Schneersohn, several times a week. There he'd stand for hours reading letters he'd received containing people's troubles, joys, and prayers.

The Rebbe passed away in 1994, but the tradition of reading prayers continues at the gravesite, referred to as the *Ohel*. Thousands of people from all over the world – including Congo, Japan, Morocco, and Nepal – come every year to seek guidance and meditate at the site, where the Rebbe is now at rest beside his father-in-law.

You don't have to be Jewish to visit the Ohel though. Corey Booker was there on the eve of his election to the US Senate. Upon arriving at the Ohel, enter the Visitor Center where a video of the Rebbe plays in the front room. Take a seat and a write a prayer request. When referring to yourself or mentioning someone else's name, use the name and mother's name (e.g. Isaac the son of Sarah). It is preferable to use one's Hebrew name. Gentiles should use their father's name.

Once done with the letter you're ready to enter the Ohel. The gravesite itself is an open-roofed granite structure with an anteroom to light candles and avail oneself of a prayerbook.

The atmosphere inside is one of hushed reverence as people stand at the waist-high wall quietly reading their letters beside the grave of the Rebbe, on the left, and his father-in-law on the right. Once you're done reading your letter, tear it up and toss it into the center.

"Just the fact that you have so many thousands of people that come here on a regular basis to pray and to pour their heart out I think is something that makes this place a special place," says Rabbi Motti Seligson, Director of Media at chabad.org.

Address 226-20 Francis Lewis Boulevard, Cambria Heights, NY 11411, +1 (718) 723-4545, www.ohelchabad.org | Getting there Take the Queens Midtown Tunnel, onto the Long Island Expressway East, continue (12.8 miles) to the Cross Island Parkway South (Exit 31S), continue (4.9 miles) to Linden Boulevard (Exit 25B), turn right onto Linden Boulevard, continue 7 blocks to 227th Street, turn left and continue 4 blocks to Francis Lewis Boulevard. Ohel Chabad Lubavitch is the house on the opposite side of the street. | Hours Open 24 hours a day except Saturdays | Tip Kosher bakeries and restaurants abound in southern Flushing, one of the best is Benjy's, home of the falafel slice (72-72 Main Street, Flushing, NY 11367).

74_ Old Quaker Meeting House

Come as a stranger and leave as a Friend

Downtown Flushing is a hive of modern commerce. However, just east of Main Street is a site steeped in history, quietude, and spirituality – the Old Quaker Meeting House.

Built in 1694, the American Colonial edifice sits with its back to the roaring traffic. You wouldn't know the rough-hewn structure was a house of worship, were it not for a sign that reads, "Friends Meeting. Silent Worship. Sundays 11 AM. All welcome," with translations in Korean, Chinese, and Spanish.

At one time the entire ground floor was used for worship. Nowadays a good portion is devoted to the history of the Religious Society of Friends, or Quakers as they are more commonly known. One wall is lined with quotes from famous Quakers, including abolitionist Isaac Hopper, who helped slaves escape as early as 1790, and Thomas Garrett, a leader in the Underground Railroad.

A torn sign reads, "INVITATION We gather in silence in the presence of God. In the silence we may worship and listen to the voice of the Spirit." Today, the Friends still gather, and you can join them. The Meeting House is not just a museum, but home to a congregation with members from all over Queens. Quakers from as far away as Alaska have been known to visit.

The spare wooden room has changed little since George Washington worshipped there. Rough-hewn wooden benches are arranged in rows. You might find a slip of paper adhered to the back of one of the benches that reads, "Integrity (honesty) is one of the Quaker Testimonies." The others include equality, peace, and care for the earth. When moved by the spirit, Friends will stand and speak. Should you enter while a Friend is speaking, wait until they are done before taking your seat.

Address 137-16 Northern Boulevard, Flushing, NY 11354, +1 (929) 251-4301, www.flushingfriends.org, flushingfriends@gmail.com | Getting there 7 train to Flushing–Main Street, then a short walk to Northern Boulevard | Hours Sun 10am–1pm | Tip Delve deeper into the roots of the Quaker movement in America at the nearby Bowne House, where John Bowne held the first Meeting in 1662 (37-01 Bowne Street, Flushing, NY 11354, www.bownehouse.org).

75__Otis & Finn Barbershop

Old-school shave and a haircut

With two locations in Long Island City, this old-fashioned barbershop is *the* place in Queens for a straight razor shave, a haircut, and a hot towel. When Shawn Dixon and Kirk Riley opened the original Court Square shop they envisioned it as a neighborhood gathering place. Local pride is paramount; the shop's slogan is "Queens y'all." That Southernism comes courtesy of Kentucky native Dixon who added a touch of hospitality with free pours of Four Roses bourbon.

Before the first location opened, Dixon and Riley gutted it down to the bare brick and left the steel beams exposed in the ceiling. With its trio of beige barber chairs, royal blue cabinets, and bathroom wallpaper featuring six-shooters and bananas, the shop's style pays homage to LIC's industrial past and its artistic present.

"Kirk and I tried to design the shops so that they were a natural fit in the community, which to us meant a combination of industrial and creative self-expression," Dixon says, pointing out that the duo's second shop on 44th Road features custom-made wallpaper that features pigs, tomatoes, and the Queensboro Bridge, and reflects the owners' love for Queens and the fact that they both grew up on farms.

"All three of us are in Queens. I walk here from Sunnyside. I love Queens," says Fred "Jedi Master Barber" Holmes, who often sports black coveralls with a leather styling holster. He knows a thing or two about the fine art of barbering.

At Otis & Finn, haircutting is most decidedly an art where attention to detail and pampering go way beyond bourbon and steaming hot towels. Working at classic Belmont barber chairs, the three stylists at the shop's original Court Square location do about 15 to 20 bespoke haircuts a day, taking their time with each and every customer.

"If you want something that's specifically tailored for you or something that's actually going to start to trend, then you would come and see us," Holmes says between shaves.

Address 45-22 Pearson Street, Long Island City, NY 11101, +1 (718) 392-2327; 11-11 44th Road, +1 (718) 433-1155, www.otisandfinn.com, otisandfinn@gmail.com | **Getting there** G or 7 train to Court House Square, E or M to Court Square-23rd Street | **Hours** Pearson Street shop Mon–Sat 10am–8pm, Sun noon–5pm; 44th Road shop Tue–Thu noon–8pm, Fri & Sat 10am–8pm | **Tip** The shop gets its hooch from nearby Court Square Wine & Spirits, which in addition to a great selection of well-priced libations features a tasting room and hosts events throughout the year, including a Puppy Party, tastings, and art shows (24-20 Jackson Avenue, Long Island City, NY 11101, www.squarewine.com).

76__ The Park at Athens Square

An ode to Grecian culture in a former playground

With dozens of Greek restaurants and souvlaki carts, Astoria has long been known as a haven for Greek culinary culture. The neighborhood's real destination for Hellenic heritage isn't a restaurant though. It's a park on the corner of 30th Avenue and 30th Street next to a public school, where a bronze statue of Athena, the Greek goddess of wisdom, towers above a sign that reads, "Athens Square." The protector of the cradle of Greek civilization beckons with an outstretched right hand. Fashioned after the Piraeus Athena (c. 350 BC), it was presented to the City of New York in 1998 by Dimitris Avramopoulos, the Mayor of Athens.

Just beyond Athena, you'll find Sophocles, the ancient Greek playwright. The author of the classics *Electra* and *Oedipus Rex* holds a tragedy mask in his left hand. At the base of the statue is an inscription that reads, "One word alone repays you for the labor of our lives – love."

Toward the back of the 0.9-acre park is a replica of a Greek amphitheater presided over by two more prominent figures in ancient Greek history, the philosophers Socrates and Aristotle.

The bronze of Socrates, designed by Anthony Frudakis, shows him seated and gesturing as if teaching. It bears the inscription, "Know thyself," the philosopher's famous motto in Greek and English. On the right you'll find a bust of Aristotle, which was bestowed upon the City of New York by Vasilios Vasilakis, Mayor of Chalkidiki, Greece, in 1998. Between the two giants of Greek culture stand three fluted Doric columns modeled after the Tholos of Athena Pronaia in Delphi.

The idea to transform a city playground into a center of Greek culture was the brainchild of Athens Square, Inc., a group of Greek immigrants from the community who commissioned Stamatios P. Lykos as the architect. Every Tuesday from 7:30pm to 9pm, the amphitheater plays host to performances by Greek musicians.

Address 30th Street and 30th Avenue, Astoria, NY 11102 | Getting there N train to 30th Avenue Station | Hours Daily 6am–9pm | Tip The feta counter at nearby Titan Foods features more than a dozen varieties and was even immortalized by Greek rapper Tiri, in his song "Feta Kai Psomi" (25-56 31st Street, Astoria, NY 11102, +1 (718) 626-7771, www.titanfoods.net).

77 __Pullis Farm Cemetery
Visit Queens' rural past in Middle Village

Parts of Queens remained quite rural up until the early 20th century, and many farms had their own cemeteries. One of the last surviving ones, Pullis Farm Cemetery, is located in Juniper Valley Park. You'll find it on the east side near 81st Street and Juniper Boulevard North.

The small graveyard where Thomas Pullis, Sr., who died in 1854, is buried lies just beyond a small grove of evergreens, oaks, and flowering cherry trees. It's closed off by a wrought-iron fence that's locked, but the gate opens just wide enough for someone svelte enough to squeeze in. Take a seat on the stone bench and ponder what life must have been like for Thomas Pullis, Sr. in 1822, when he purchased his 32-acre farm, which ran along Dry Harbor Road south to Furmanville Avenue.

Pullis transported his wares to Manhattan's Catherine Market via ferry. On the way, he and his fellow farmers would often stop by a roadhouse on Brooklyn & Jamaica Turnpike just east of 69th Street for much needed refreshment. The tavern would become venerable German restaurant Niederstein's in 1888. Sadly, Niederstein's was torn down in 2005 and replaced by an Arby's fast food restaurant.

When Thomas Pullis, Sr. died in 1854 his three sons inherited the farm, and his will stipulated that the cemetery was never to be sold.

For many years, the Pullis Farm Cemetery was in disrepair but, thanks to the efforts of local resident Ed Shusterich, it was restored in 1994. He solicited donations of plants, trees, and topsoil from local nurseries, planted the evergreens, oaks, white birch, and flowering apples and cherries that surround the cemetery. In 1997, Lutheran All Faiths Cemetery donated a new gravestone, a statue of Miss Autumn to honor the Pullis Family.

The roadhouse that became Niederstein's may have fallen victim to so-called progress, but Pullis Farm Cemetery remains. No doubt Thomas Pullis, Sr. would be glad his dying wishes were respected.

Address Juniper Valley Park, 81st Street and Juniper Boulevard North, Middle Village, NY 11379 | Getting there R train to Woodhaven Boulevard then Q29 bus to Dry Harbor Road and 63rd Avenue | Hours Daily 6am – 9pm | Tip Continue your exploration of neighborhood history with a visit to Trinity Lutheran Church, which was founded in 1851, burned down in 1863, and was once more consumed by fire in 1977. Two church bells – one from 1895 and one from 1908 – are all that remain of the original church (63-70 Dry Harbor Road, Middle Village, NY 11379).

78___Q.E.D.

Show and tell for grown-ups

Quod erat demonstrandum, a Latin phrase usually abbreviated Q.E.D. and which means "thus it has been demonstrated," typically appears at the bottom of mathematical proofs. You don't normally see it at the top of performance spaces. Then again, Q.E.D. A Place to Show & Tell, which offers everything from standup comedy and open mic nights to classes that run the gamut from salsa dancing to home brewing, isn't a typical performance space.

"We're a place to show and tell," says Kambri Krews, who opened Q.E.D. in 2014. "So if some people want to think it means Queens Ed., then sure, there's a double meaning," Krews says.

The course offerings include a curriculum as diverse as Queens itself, with classes in embroidery, sketch comedy writing, and anthropomorphic insect shadowbox making. You can learn about honey harvesting from Astoria beekeeper Nick Hoefly. Historian Jason D. Antos has given a lecture on Astoria's Hell Gate Bridge in celebration of its 100th anniversary, and Richard Melnick hosted a *Beatles at Shea* retrospective. "We really like to highlight what's great about Queens," says Krews. That greatness includes local comedians like Anthony Devito, Jon Fish, and Ted Alexander.

Krews, who has a background in storytelling and did comedy booking for 92Y Tribeca, decided to open Q.E.D. after she and her husband realized there was really no place for them to perform in their Astoria neighborhood.

"This is my home, this is my neighborhood. I've never lived anywhere my whole life as long as I've lived here. I want to give back to this community," Krews says.

So what's the strangest class ever taught at Q.E.D.? "Make Your Own Stone Tools for the Zombiepocalypse," is a strong contender. The teacher, Krews says, is an archeologist, who works in Africa. "So he's teaching you something really serious and real but making it fun.

Address 27-16 23rd Avenue, Astoria, NY 11105, +1 (347) 451-3873, www.qedastoria.com, QEDAstoria@gmail.com | **Getting there** N train to Ditmars Boulevard | **Hours** Sun noon–11pm, Mon & Tue 6–11pm, Wed noon–11pm, Thu noon–midnight, Fri noon–1am | **Tip** The iconic Unisphere lies at the heart of Q.E.D.'s logo. In the summertime, the fountains in front of the actual Unisphere come on in Flushing Meadows–Corona Park, providing a cooling playground and rainbows around the beloved, glittering steel globe (www.nycgovparks.org/parks/flushing-meadows-corona-park).

79_ Queens County Farm Museum

Oldest working farm in New York State

Two hundred years ago, much of Queens was used for farming. Today, only two farms remain: one is on a rooftop in Long Island City, and the other is the Queens County Farm Museum located in the heart of Floral Park.

At 47 acres, the Queens County Farm Museum dwarfs its LIC cousin by about 50 times. It's the oldest continually farmed site in New York State, dating to the 1600s. In 1697, John Harrison sold the farm to Elbert Adriance, whose family owned the property for more than 100 years. The Adriance Farmhouse, the centerpiece of the museum's farm complex, was first built as a three-room Dutch farmhouse in 1772.

By 1900, the farm was owned by Daniel Stattel, who turned it into the county's second-largest farm. He was a major player in the golden age of truck farming, sending record tons of crops to market.

In 1926, the farm was sold to Pauline Reisman, who in turn sold it to New York State, which used it to supply produce to Creedmoor State Hospital until 1975. While Reisman did not contribute anything agriculturally, her sale of the farm spared it from the rampant development that was taking place in Queens in the 1920s.

Today, the property is not just a museum, it's very much a working farm with everything from Italian honeybees to heritage breed pigs that are fed spent grain from Ridgewood's Bridge & Tunnel Brewery.

"We like to feature the heritage breeds because they're closer to the types of animals that would have been raised historically," says Ali Abate, the farm's director of education.

If you visit the farm in late summer, be sure to grab some tomatoes from the farmstand and a dozen farm-fresh eggs, which come in shades of white, brown, and even blue. from the gift shop.

Address 73-50 Little Neck Parkway, Floral Park, NY 11004, +1 (718) 347-3276, www.queensfarm.org, info@queensfarm.org | Getting there F train to Union Turnpike–Kew Gardens Station, then Q 46 bus to Union Turnpike/252nd Street | Hours Daily 10am–5pm | Tip Continue your exploration of Queens' farming history in Douglaston at the Allen-Beville House, one of the borough's few surviving 19th-century farmhouses (29 Center Drive, Douglaston, NY 11363).

80 Queens Night Market

International nightlife under the stars and tents

Not far from the Unisphere – the towering steel globe from the 1964 World's Fair that has come to represent the diverse nature of Queens – stands another testament to diversity: the Queens International Night Market. Enter and you'll be greeted by dozens of tents featuring international delicacies, ranging from Chinese barbecued squid on a stick to Peruvian ceviche.

Since it began in 2015 the open-air market has represented cuisines from more than 70 countries, says its founder John Wang. "Our goal is to have a tent for every country represented in New York City," he says of the market that draws thousands of hungry folks on Saturday nights.

Wang's parents are from Taiwan and he has many fond childhood memories of summers spent at Taiwanese night markets. Wang is quick to point out though that his brainchild is not an Asian night market. "The twist on it is that we're in Queens and New York City, the most diverse place in the world, so we decided to make it international."

Only at the QINM will you find Greek baklava next to Dominican mofongo. Karl Balls, a purveyor of the octopus fritters known as takoyaki continues to draw huge lines as do the Chinese squid skewers from Gi Hin Mama Food. Myo Lin Thway the chef behind Burmese Bites has been kneading and stretching gossamer thin palatha and stuffing it with chicken keema since the market's inception. His pride for his homeland and home borough are underscored by his team's uniform. In a tip of the hat to the Mets they each sport blue baseball caps with orange script that reads "Burmese Bites." New additions this year include The Malaysian Project's Ramly burger, a hamburger wrapped in a fried egg and seasoned with curry.

"Queens to me is just all about diversity, it's not supercrowded, it's not superexpensive yet, at least most of it," Wang says. "It still has a kind of like an underdog status."

Address 47-01 111th Street, Corona, NY 11368, www.queensnightmarket.com | Getting there 7 train to 111th Street | Hours Apr–Oct Sat 6pm–midnight, check website for exact dates | Tip Not enough to eat at the market? Head to Tortas Neza, where the specialty is giant overstuffed Mexican tortas, including the Puma which is larger than your head and includes a chorizo omelet (96-15 Roosevelt Avenue, Corona, NY 11368).

81__The Ramp

Hey Ho, let's go to the birthplace of American Punk

The most distinguishing characteristic of The Ramp used to be a rainbow colored Slinky entwined with the barbed wire atop a fence surrounding the roof. Now closed, the roof was once a hangout for punk rock pioneers The Ramones. Today, a mural by Lower East Side artist Ori Carino marks where punk rock came kicking and screaming into staid 1970s Queens. It was painted to commemorate the 40th anniversary of The Ramones' first album.

Before they became The Ramones, Jeffrey Hyman (Joey), Douglas Colvin (Dee Dee), Tamás Erdélyi, (Tommy), and John Cummings (Johnny) all hung out there. They met at Forest Hills High School, and Tommy formed the band in 1974. Their fake surnames came from one used by Sir Paul McCartney to check into hotels: Paul Ramon.

"The Ramones all originated from Forest Hills and kids who grew up there either became musicians, degenerates, or dentists," read their first press release. "The Ramones are a little of each. Their sound is not unlike a fast drill on a rear molar."

"We would regroup there after hitching to Rockaway Beach to hear everyone's crazy stories and see who didn't make it back," recalled Mickey Leigh, Joey's brother, in "I Slept With Joey Ramone."

Before Hilly Kristal, the owner of CBGBs, would tell Joey, "Nobody's gonna like you guys, but I'll have you back," he played his first gigs at Coventry in Sunnyside, Queens. So did many other 1970s acts, including The Dictators and The New York Dolls, who also would go onto play the Lower East Side club. Some, like Kiss, even went on to achieve greater fame.

"The New York rock scene of the 1970s was The Ramones, Kiss, and The New York Dolls. They all really came from the same neighborhood. Forest Hills High School and Newtown High School are a 15-minute walk from each other," says Andy Shernoff, founder of The Dictators, who grew up in Jackson Heights. "Queens is the borough of rock."

Address 66th Avenue between 99th and 102nd Streets, Rego Park, NY 11374 | **Getting there** R or M train to 67th Avenue | **Hours** Unrestricted, viewable from outside only | **Tip** Nearby in Forest Hills on Ascan Avenue close to to Burns street is a mural by Crisp and Praxis depicting history of a different sort: the community's founders Russell Sage, Margaret Olivia Slocum Sage, Ascan Backus, Grosvenor Atterbury, and Frederick Law Olmsted, Jr.

82 Resobox

Catch the vibes of Japanese culture

You might think you'd have to travel to Tokyo to study Japanese painting, flower arranging, and swordsmanship, but in the World's Borough you need look no further than Queens Plaza. That's where you'll find Resobox, where every aspect of Japanese culture resonates.

"Resobox was a name created from the words resonate and box," says Sunnyside resident Takashi Ikezawa. "We resonate with people in New York City through Japanese culture." The concept was created by Ikezawa's friend, New York City composer and videographer Fumio Tashiro in August 2009. In the wake of the devastating Japanese earthquake that took place in March 2011, Tashiro and Ikezawa worked to refine Resobox. In June 2011 their efforts led to Resobox's home in Long Island City.

Today Resobox's classes run the gamut from workshops in *ikebana*, or Japanese flower arranging and bonsai to such martial arts as *iaido*, a Japanese sword technique that is also used as a form of meditation. There are also classes in drawing *manga* or Japanese cartoons, and once a month there is a two-hour cooking class.

The kitchen offers several types of ramen, including rich pork-based *tonkotsu* and spicy miso. Among the decidedly Japanese appetizers are tako wasabi, or raw octopus with Japanese horseradish, and *natto tofu*, blocks of firm tofu with pungent fermented soybeans. Five types of sake are available and specialty soft drinks include *kurogama* or black sesame latte.

Resobox's art shows have ranged from the paper art of Sam Ita, influenced by manga and Western literature, to ceramics from Yasumitsu Morito. One of the most popular shows over the years has been the annual World Amigurumi Exhibition, which has been taking place since 2014, where thousands of fanciful crocheted creatures crowd the space. In case you're wondering, Resobox also offers a class in how to make them. It takes place every Tuesday night.

Address 41-26 27th Street, Long Island City, NY 11101, +1 (718) 784-3680, www.resobox.org, info@resobox.com | **Getting there** N, W, or 7 train to Queensboro Plaza | **Hours** Daily noon–10pm, closed 4–5pm | **Tip** Next door to Resobox, you'll find Seito New York, an emporium that specializes in all manner of Japanese restaurant equipment: sushi knives and cleavers, chopsticks, and soup bowls (41-26 27th Street, Long Island City, www.seito-newyork.com).

83 _ Riis Park Beach Bazaar

A taste of Brooklyn beside the beach in Queens

Odds are that when New York City Parks Commissioner Robert Moses planned the Art Deco beach houses of Riis Park in the 1930s, he never imagined a mobile barbecue rig would sit smoking away beside the fluted columns of Bay 9. The rig belongs to Fletcher's Brooklyn Barbecue and cooks up pork and brisket. It's just one of several food offerings at Riis Park Beach Bazaar, which took over the concessions at the 85-year-old park in 2015.

Next to Fletcher's stand, find a taste of New England at Rockaway Clam Bar, which offers little necks on the half shell, lobster rolls, and fried clam sandwiches. The specialty at Ed & Bev's is Coney dogs: wieners topped with chili, raw onions, and mustard. Despite the name, the frankfurters are not a specialty of Brooklyn's Coney Island, but rather a Detroit delicacy. Bolivian Llama Party offers a decadent 10-ingredient *sandwich de chola*, packed with pork, bacon, housemade cheese, *aji panka* peppers, and roasted garlic, among other things. Adult refreshment in the form of a Ginni Hendricks – green tea, black tea, lemonade, and Hendrick's gin – is available at the Riis Point Bar.

Even though it's in Queens, the Brooklyn connection at Riis is quite strong. Ample Hills Creamery, which scoops decadent ice cream flavors like Ooey Gooey Butter Cake, takes its name from a line in Walt Whitman's poem, "Crossing Brooklyn Ferry." Look northwest, and you can see another crossing to the County of Kings, the Marine Parkway Bridge, which links Riis to Floyd Bennett Field.

If you're coordinated enough, try eating your lunch in one of the hammocks that line the boardwalk. Pick up some handmade jewelry or beachwear at the small artisan market.

Riis Park Beach Bazaar also plays host to many free summer concerts, including the three-day Rock! Away! Music Fest, which takes place every July and hosts a beach volleyball league every Wednesday.

Address 167-02 Rockaway Beach Boulevard, Rockaway Park, NY 11694, www.riisparkbeachbazaar.com, info@rpbeachbazaar.com | Getting there M or R train to Woodhaven Bouelvard then Q-53 bus to Beach 116 Street/Rockaway Beach Boulevard then Q-35 to Jacob Riis Park Road/Basketball Courts | Hours Daily 11am–10pm | Tip Before hitting the beach and the concessions enjoy a game of golf at the adjacent Riis Park Golf Course.

84 Rocket Park

Blast off into the history of the space program

Not far from the Unisphere, the glittering stainless-steel representation of planet Earth that is a legacy of the 1964–65 World's Fair, stand several spacecraft that helped kick off the Space Race. Depending on your vantage point in Flushing Meadows Corona Park, it can be incongruous to see the glittering machines towering above the trees. You'll find the pair of rockets – a Gemini Titan II and Mercury Atlas-D – in the aptly named Rocket Park, just outside the New York Hall of Science.

Next to the rockets is a Saturn V F-1 engine. The F-1 engine is one of the most powerful rocket engines ever built, producing as much thrust as all three space shuttle main engines combined. As you walk around the Gemini Titan II, a second-generation intercontinental ballistic missile used to launch the two-man Gemini spacecraft, imagine what it was like to float above the Earth's atmosphere in such close quarters.

Rocket Park also features a Man on the moon Timeline, which traces the history of man's conquest of the Moon from ancient times to President John F. Kennedy's historic 1961 speech to Congress that declared, "No single space project in this period will be more impressive to mankind, or more important for the long-range exploration of space…" to Neil Armstrong's historic walk on the lunar surface.

Explore the principles of rocket science – propulsion, thrust, gravity, escape velocity, launch window – as you putt your way through the adjacent Rocket Park Mini Golf, which features a hole called Blast Off! that challenges visitors to shoot the ball up an inclined ramp with enough velocity to "blast off" a model rocket up a gantry.

"We really enjoyed the challenge of bringing 'rocket science' down to earth in a way that would excite and delight people of all ages, even while they learned real physics!" said Lee H. Skolnick, of Lee H. Skolnick Architecture + Design.

Address 47-01 111th Street, Corona, NY 11368, +1 (718) 699-0005, www.nysci.org/
rocket-park, info@nysci.org | Getting there 7 train to 111th Street | Hours Mon–Fri
9:30am–5pm, Sat & Sun 10am–6pm | Tip While you're in Flushing Meadows–Corona
Park, pay a visit to the Queens Zoo, which houses everything from bison and bears to
egrets and sea lions (53-51 111th Street, Corona, NY 11368, www.queenszoo.com).

85 Rokhat Kosher Bakery

Bukharian bread and culture in Rego Park

When you hear the words "kosher bakery," the first thing you think of is braided loaves of *challah*. Rokhat, which lies in the heart of Queens' Bukharian Jewish community does make a braided loaf – *bukhara* – but it's round, the braided golden circumference surrounding a dimple that bears a spiral marked by tiny pinholes. With the exception of one rectangular loaf, all of the breads here are round, just like those from the 10 bakeries that surrounded the Samekhov's family home back in Bukhara, Uzbekistan.

Before he came to America in 1992, Syleman Samekhov had a photography studio. When he came to the States, he opened the bakery armed with knowledge he had picked up from watching the local bakers back home, as his son, Roshiel, recalls.

Today the bakery produces between 500 and 800 loaves a day. The ornate *bukhara*; *chak chak,* a Tashkent-style sesame-studded loaf with a swirled surface; and Samarkand, which resembles a giant bialy, are the top three sellers. Many of the breads contain ornate designs in their center, including a Shabbat loaf that bears a Star of David. "In Bukhara, they do all kinds of designs," Roshiel says. "Whatever you tell them, they can write."

All of the breads are cooked in giant tandoor ovens imported from Uzbekistan. The loaves are stuck to the walls of the ovens where they bake for half an hour. Next door, there's a smaller tandoor where savory lamb *samsa* are baked in a similar fashion. For years the bakery used an oven from Uzbekistan but found it difficult to work with and switched to an Indian tandoor. "We got it right here in Queens," Roshiel says when asked if the oven was imported.

The workers, who are in and out of the blazing hot tandoors all day, wear white towels on their head to help them cope with the heat. "That's why I don't go to the *banya* because it's here," Roshiel says when asked to recommend a Russian bathhouse."

Address 65-43 Austin Street, Rego Park, NY 11374, +1 (718) 897-4493 | Getting there R or M train to 63rd Drive, then walk south on 63rd to Austin Street | Hours Sun – Fri 7am – 8pm | Tip Now that you've found the best bread in Rego Park, find some smoked fish to fill it at the gigantic Russian supermarket NetCost (97-10 Queens Boulevard, Rego Park, NY 11374, www.netcostmarket.com).

86_Rubie's Costume Co.

Chills and thrills in Richmond Hill's land of Halloween

If you've ever bought a pirate costume or a Minions outfit for your kid or your dog, odds are it came from Rubie's, the world's largest costume manufacturer, in operation since 1984.

Open Rubie's doors and two purple dragons will usher you inside to a land where it's always Halloween. "Welcome to Rubies," they say with a puff of smoke. A mask of President Donald Trump sits beside the South Park Kids and scary clowns. The Tin Man, a kid-friendly classic, abuts the gruesome visage of Billy the Puppet from the *Saw* horror movies.

There's a sleeping ogre who sits with his hands on his knees, a presence to be reckoned with. But there's so much to look at, from $1,000 collectible Darth Vader costumes to SpongeBob piñatas, so nobody will blame you if you don't notice the ogre at first.

"I love those little people. I really think they're neat. I'll have them home for dinner 'cause they're really good to eat," he mumbles before rising to his full height of 15 feet! "Oh, hi! Didn't see you come in. You're at one of the funniest places on the planet – Rubie's Costumes," he announces.

As you make your way through the aisles with 1960s hippy getups and warrior princess outfits, you'll hear a creepy lullaby. A gray ghoul in a rocking chair cradling a zombie baby is the source. Nearby is an electric chair, whose occupant smokes and pops.

When Ruben and Tillie, the parents of Rubie's current president Marc Beige, opened Rubie's in 1951, it was a candy store. They later branched out into selling gags and Halloween items. "As Halloween grew, it pushed out the candy store," Beige recalls.

Beige still dresses up for Halloween: Darth Vader for the past two years, though the 66-year-old says he will probably mix it up this year and go as a superhero. Ask him about Rubie's most unusual costume, and he won't hesitate to tell you: The Fruit of the Loom Guys.

Address 120-08 Jamaica Avenue, Richmond Hill, NY 11418, +1 (718) 846-1008, www.rubies.com | Getting there E train to Jamaica–Van Wyck | Hours Mon–Sat 10am–6pm | Tip Stay on target by honing your archery skills at Pro Line Archery Lanes, where everyone from bow hunters to competitive archers comes to enjoy this centuries-old sport (95-11 101st Avenue, Ozone Park, NY 11416, www.prolinearchery.com).

87__Rudar Miner's Club
Eat and drink like a Croatian coal miner in Astoria

Before you enter this soccer club, take note of the logo on the green awning. A ball and the year 1977 sit above a crossed hammer and pick axe. Below is the club's official name, United Miners S.C. Rudar.

From the early afternoon into the evening the old men play cards – briškula and tressette – some chattering in Labinjonski. It's the dialect of their forefathers, coal miners originally from the town of Labin, Croatia. On the wall opposite the bar are two clocks, one showing New York time and the other Labin time, which is six hours ahead.

The club has about 150 members and most, but not all, are from Labin, says its treasurer Angela Pamic. "It's not a prerequisite to be from Labin," Pamic says. Nor is it a prerequisite to be a miner, although that is what the word "rudar" means.

In 1977, a group of unmarried men, immigrants from Labin, who were crazy about soccer pooled their money together to open the club. "European men of that age don't know how to cook," Pamic says by way of explaining the homestyle restaurant in the basement. Take a seat by the fireplace, which features a drawing of a smiling rudar complete with head lamp on the mantle. Dig deep into a menu of such specialties as Istrian *pršut*, the Croatian cousin of Italian prosciutto, and *njoki sa zvacetom istarski* (homemade gnocchi with veal sauce). Bring a coal miner's appetite or some friends because the appetizer portion of gnocchi bathed in a homey red sauce is huge and perfect for sharing. Pamic's favorite is *fuži*, a bowtie pasta in the same rich veal sauce.

In the beginning Rudar was members only, but more and more people kept bringing friends to try the homemade pastas, and eventually the club opened to the public. The restaurant that popularized the club is still going strong, the soccer teams not so much. "We used to have a couple of soccer teams, right now we just have the 40 and up soccer," Pamic says.

Address 34-01 45th Street, Astoria, NY 11101, +1 (718) 786-5833 | **Getting there** R or M train to Steinway Street | **Hours** Tue–Thu 3–10pm, Fri & Sat 3–11pm, Sun noon–10pm | **Tip** Why not end your trip to Eastern Europe in high style with a nightcap at the swanky Astor Room (35-11 35th Avenue, Astoria, NY 11106, www.astorroom.com)?

88 Rudolph Valentino's Mansion

Bayside oasis of Hollywood's original sex symbol

At first glance, the sumptuous three-story mansion, located next to the Clearview Park Golf Course and a stone's throw from the approach to the Throgs Neck Bridge, might be mistaken for a New York State Parks building. After all, it bears the agency's green leaf logo. The mansion's claim to fame is that it was once owned by American cinema's first heartthrob, Rudolph Valentino. The stately domicile goes back to the era of silent films in American cinema, when many actors, including Rudolph Valentino and Charlie Chaplin, called the area home.

Valentino, an Italian immigrant born Rodolfo Alfonso Raffaello Pierre Filibert Guglielmi di Valentina d'Antonguella, was famous for playing Sheik Ahmed Ben Hassan in the 1921 silent film, *The Sheik*. No doubt he viewed his Bayside home much like the "blessed oasis" that sets the stage for that film. Back when Valentino set down roots in northeast Queens, it was a celebrity haven. He and Babe Ruth were both members of the prestigious Oakland Golf Club, which was razed to make way for the Throgs Neck Bridge. In the 1920s, the golf course that abuts the mansion was a retreat known as the Clearview Golf and Yacht Club.

Today, the mansion, with its spectacular views of Little Bay and the East River, is home to Vivo Mediterranean Grille. There's little indication of the building's most famous resident. You might think that the gold tile-work letter "V" framed in laurel leaves inlaid in the floor is was put there by the Latin Lover, but it was put there by a former restaurant tenant, Valentino's On The Green. On top of the mantel of the original fireplace sits a photo of Hollywood's original sex symbol, but not as the Sheik. In his open-necked white dress shirt Valentino bears a passing resemblance to Jordan Belfort, Hollywood's somewhat less beloved Wolf of Wall Street, who also called Bayside home.

Address 201-10 Cross Island Parkway, Bayside, NY 11360, +1 (718) 352-2300, www.vivobayside.com | Getting there 7 train to Flushing–Main Street then Q16 bus to Cross Island Parkway and 201st Street | Hours Mansion is always viewable from the outside; restaurant Tue–Thu 5–10pm, Fri & Sat 5–11pm, Sun 11:30am–3pm & 4–9pm | Tip Not only was Bayside once the home of Hollywood's first male sex symbol, it was once the residence of its first femme fatale, Theda Bara, a silent film star who pioneered the role of the Vamp, a woman who seduces men and causes them to leave their families (209-07 43rd Avenue, Bayside, NY 11360).

89__Schmidt's Candy Store

A sweet trip to the past under the J train

This 92-year-old candy store greets you with an intoxicating aroma of chocolate. Many of the treats, like the chocolate-covered nuts, pineapple wedges, raspberry jellies, caramels, and mints, have been sold since Margie Schmidt's immigrant German grandfather opened the shop back in 1925.

Save for the street, which used to be cobblestone, little has changed. As the J train rumbles overhead, Margie kibitzes with customers and hand-dips chocolates using the same methods her grandfather did. The sign outside reads, "home-made," and they're not kidding. "I don't make a raisin. I'm not growing a peanut, but the marshmallow, the marzipan, the coconut are all made with these 10 fingers," Margie says.

She took over the shop from her mother in 1986, but the 58-year-old has been working there since she was a little girl, when there was an ice cream parlor on every block between 75th and 111th Street. In fact, her family's shop once had an ice cream counter. Several holes in the floor mark the space where the stools once stood.

"When you were little you put eyes and bows on the bunnies," Margie says recalling Easters of years past. The holiday remains the busiest time at this Woodhaven institution. "When you turned 10 years old, you had to start putting chicks and rabbits in a bag and counting to 12," she says with a laugh. "If you could count to 12, you got a job here – that was the rule."

Her lifelong personal favorite chocolate is a half-dipped graham cracker, but the treat was not sold in the shop. Margie would listen for her father to come home at night, and he would place a package on the top shelf of the cabinet. "In the morning I'd run downstairs and pull down the box," Margie says. "Sometimes they were covered with dark chocolate, and I'd shove them back in the cabinet because I was disappointed," says the master chocolatier who to this day prefers milk chocolate over dark.

Address 94-15 Jamaica Avenue, Woodhaven, NY 11421, +1 (718) 846-9326, www.schmidtscandy.com, schmidtscandy@yahoo.com | **Getting there** J train to Woodhaven Boulevard | **Hours** Tue–Sat 11am–6pm, closed July and Aug | **Tip** Frederick Christ Trump, father of US President Donald Trump, was born in Woodhaven in 1905. You'll find a sign commemorating this fact in the parking lot of Compare Foods Supermarket, which the elder Trump built (77-20 Jamaica Avenue, Woodhaven, NY 11421, www.comparesupermarkets.com).

90__ Scrabble Street Sign
The birthplace of America's most popular word game

In the heart of the Jackson Heights, you'll find the Community United Methodist Church. Built in 1919, the stone structure stands at 81st Street and 35th Avenue. On that corner is a street sign that commemorates a piece of history: not the church's founding, but rather the birth of the popular word game, Scrabble.

In 1933, Alfred Mosher Butts, an unemployed architect and congregant of the church created a word game, noting that "…there is one thing that keeps word games from being as popular as card games: they have no score." Butts originally called it Lexiko and derived the letter distribution by analyzing *The New York Times*.

Contrary to popular opinion, "scrabble," is a real word, which means "to grope frantically." At first, Butts did indeed grope frantically as game makers rejected his creation. Then he met a game-loving entrepreneur, James Brunot, who backed the game. The two teamed up and rented an abandoned schoolhouse where they turned out 12 sets an hour, stamping letters on wooden tiles one at a time. In 1948, they trademarked the name "Scrabble," and today it is found in one out of three American homes.

The 35th Avenue street sign earns 14 points. It was first installed in 1995, but it was vandalized in 2008, says Queens Borough Historian Jack Eichenbaum, who is himself a competitive Scrabble player. "It's very dear to me as a Queens historian and a Scrabble player," he says. "I've often taken visiting players there."

In 2011, New York City Council member Daniel Dromm returned the sign to its rightful place. "The creator of Scrabble and the residents of Jackson Heights share certain traits: they are creative, persistent, and unwilling to give up easily," said Barbaralee Diamonstein-Spielvogel, who at the time was chair of the New York City's Landmarks Preservation Center. Were it possible to play the words "Jackson Heights," they would garner 34 points.

Address 81st Street and 35th Avenue/81-10 35th Avenue, Jackson Heights, NY 11372 | Getting there 7 train to 82nd Street–Jackson Heights | Hours Unrestricted | Tip The garden in the nearby St. Mark's Episcopal Church is a lovely place to sit and perhaps even enjoy a board game (33-50 82nd Street, Jackson Heights, NY 11372, www.stmarks.net).

91 The Secret Theatre

Center for Shakespeare hidden in plain sight

Eight years ago when British-born Richard Mazda founded The Secret Theatre, the 99-seat house's Long Island City neighborhood was still *terra incognita* for most New Yorkers. Today the theater, which produces everything from Shakespeare to musicals and children's shows, lies in the shadow of rapidly rising residential towers.

"When I was founding the theater that book, *The Secret*, was everywhere, everybody loved that book and so that was in my mind," recalls Mazda, the theater's artistic director. The idea that some of the best places are hidden gems also resonated with Mazda. "Some of the best destinations that you go in New York are either secrets or they're hard to find."

The name was also a bit of an inside joke, Mazda recalls. "Where is it? Don't know. What do they do? We have no idea?" What they do there is host all manner of productions, including such Shakespeare works as *Henry V*, *Julius Caesar*, and most recently *King Lear*. Mazda, a self-described "Shakespeare geek," was especially proud to have renowned character actor Austin Pendleton in the lead role. "We try to do it at the highest level we can according to our budgets and means," Mazda says of the Shakespeare productions. He has also written two children's shows, *Pirate Pete* and *Princess Particular*, which are performed monthly.

Musicals also play a large role in the theater's line-up. Everything from such classics as *Cabaret* and *You're a Good Man, Charlie Brown* to newer works such as *Grindhouse Musical* and *Secret Burlesque Wants You* have graced the stage.

"People come for the first time and they say, 'It was so hard to find,' and I know that that's really not true," Mazda says with a laugh. "It's not hard to find, we have seven subway lines here."

So even though LIC's no secret anymore and the theater's easy to find, the real secret is quality theater steps away from the 7 train.

Address 44-02 23rd Street, Long Island City, NY 11101, +1 (718) 392-0722, www.secrettheatre.com | Getting there 7, E, M, or R train to Court Square–23rd Street Station | Hours See website for scheduled performances and tickets | Tip For a great farm-to-table brunch chef Alex Schindler's LIC Market is not to be missed (21-52 44th Drive, Long Island City, NY 11101, www.licmarket.com).

92 Smiling Hogshead Ranch

Get back to the land at this urban garden in LIC

Despite the name, Smiling Hogshead Ranch has no livestock. It is a farm, though an urban one, located on a patch of abandoned rail yard at the intersection of Pearson and Skillman, with Manhattan's skyline beaming in the distance.

A group of locals who care about protecting the environment and growing local foods founded Smiling Hogshead Ranch in 2011, eventually transforming the patch of urban wasteland to a vest-pocket oasis with 14 beds and a grapevine. The farm grows everything from basil, thyme, and lavender to carrots, squash, and cherry tomatoes. A teal-and-white sign sporting a smiling cartoon pig gives a clue to the farm's name. In 2011, the founders were cleaning up the former brownfield of debris and found two plastic bags. "One had a pig's skull in it, and one had a butcher's knife in it," says Board Member Colin Samuel. "So that became the smiling hog."

Since the tract belongs to New York's Metropolitan Transportation Authority, the urban farmers can't sell their crops. Instead members pay fees to buy seeds and tools. One thing that isn't purchased is soil. They make it through a process known as a biodynamic windrow. Eight tons of food scraps – the equivalent of two elephants – from GrowNYC's greenmarket composting project are brought to the lot twice a year. "We rebuild the soil from scratch. So a space that had no soil before now has reusable, replenishable soil for the future," Samuel points out.

The original project started small, and more people have become involved today. Even local elected officials recognize the fact that the garden is now an important part of the community.

You too can get your hands dirty and join that good work. Each spring, you can join Terrific Tuesdays, when members and guests harvest the produce and then enjoy a potluck dinner together.

Address 25-30 Skillman Avenue, Long Island City, NY 11101, +1 (347) 509-4464, www.smiling-hogshead-ranch.tumblr.com, smilinghogsheadranch@gmail.com | Getting there 7 train to Hunters Point Avenue | Hours Mon–Fri 11am–3pm, Sat & Sun 9am–5pm | Tip Housed in what was once a greeting card factory, Long Island City's Flux Factory plays host to and sponsors all manner of experimental art, including Cinema Flux and Self Storage, which turns storage units over to artists to create exhibits (39-31 29th Street, Long Island City, NY 11101, www.fluxfactory.org).

93__ Spaghetti Park Bocce Court

Watching world-class bocce on warm summer nights

Summer doesn't start in this corner of Queens until the boys come out to play in Spaghetti Park. The game in question is bocce, once the sole province of older Italian men. These days the players, each a crack shot at the game whose object is toss one's team's balls – red or green after the Italian flag – closest to the smaller ball, known as the *pallino*, are a mix of Italians and Dominicans.

"It's been there forever," says Vinnie Barbaccia, co-owner of The Lemon Ice King of Corona of the court that was constructed after World War II. "That was the thing, especially if you were from the neighborhood, you knew you didn't go on the bocce court. That was set aside for just the old Italian guys really, the serious players."

These days, the games are still serious if you call stakes of $5 serious, and you probably still won't get invited to play, but exceptions have been known to have been made. Better to grab an ice and enjoy the show. Red and green balls clack against each other as the players call out "lunga" and "corte" in Italian, denoting long and short shots that have missed the mark. "Sácalo," or "get it out" in Spanish is a common cry when players want to displace the other team's ball.

One thing that hasn't changed is quibbling over who's closest to the *pallino*. Some of the men use an antenna to measure the disputed distance, while others prefer an old-fashioned hinged carpenter's ruler. And then there's Nico, the one-time champion, an irascible white-haired octagenarian, who loves to fight over points. "He's still very good, he's a world-class player," Barbaccia says.

The park was built to honor Private William F. Moore (1897 – 1918), a Marine killed in battle during World War I. These days, it is maintained by Anthony "Tough Tony" Federici, a captain in the Genovese mafia family and owner of the adjacent Park Side restaurant.

Address 107-06 Corona Avenue, Corona, NY 11368, www.joyofbocce.com/Corona.ivnu | **Getting there** 7 train to 103rd Street–Corona Plaza | **Hours** If the weather's good, the boys will likely be there playing. | **Tip** For the freshest mozzarella around with a side of Italian American hospitality, be sure to visit Leo's Latticini (46-02 104th Street, Corona, NY 11368).

94_ Steinway & Sons Factory

Pianos still handcrafted by the masters

Every Queens resident has heard of Steinway Street. And everybody – Queens resident or not – has heard of Steinway pianos. What many don't know is that the street's history and the piano's are intertwined. Steinway Street was the heart of a company town that Steinway & Sons founded in the late 1800s. These days, the company still makes pianos in the far reaches of northern Astoria, using the same processes Henry E. Steinway pioneered when the plant opened in 1870.

Tour participants get a close-up look at the piano-making process. Guides are quick to point out: "The only piano that exists is a Steinway piano; we call others piano-shaped objects." Do not touch the wood – you don't want a splinter from "rock maple."

The wood is harvested green, cured, and used to form the piano's body. This vital first step in the nine-month process of creating a Steinway is the first stop on the tour. To create the body of a concert grand, a team of six men work in perfectly choreographed silence to layer and glue together 19 sheets of wood. The team has a scant 20 minutes for the entire process, which concludes with placing the 400-pound stack into a piano-shaped vise where it is pressed and bent into shape.

"If the Steinway brothers came back today, they'd be able to work this line," the guide points out. The commitment to quality is everywhere, borne out by signs like: "You don't have to love the work, but you're addicted to the results."

Nowhere is the commitment to craftsmanship more in evidence than the Action Department, where dozens of men and women fabricate the felt-clad bass and treble hammers by hand. Each tour guest receives a hammer as a souvenir. What you will really come away with, though, is a deep appreciation for why Steinway pioneered the phrase "Made in the USA," and why it has had such a special place in the world of music for almost 150 years.

Address 1 Steinway Place, Astoria, NY 11105, +1 (718) 721-2600, info@steinway.com | Getting there N train to Ditmars Boulevard | Hours Tours: Sept–July Tue 9:30am–noon; open for scheduled tours only; reserve in advance via phone or e-mail | Tip Back in the day, Rosario Dimarco had a pizzeria near the Steinway factory. These days, Rosario's continues to serve some of the best pizza and Italian sandwiches around (22-55 31st Street, Astoria, NY 11105, www.rosariosastoria.us).

95__Sugar Club

Part grocery, part café, all Thai

When Chirawat "Jimmy" Withanwattana came to America in 2008 from Bangkok, the first place he visited was Sugar Club. He sought a job and a place to live, and the shop's bulletin board was well known as a source for both in the Thai community.

If you're visiting Elmhurst's Little Bangkok, you'd do well to make Sugar Club your first stop too. When it opened in 1989, the tiny shop sold Thai videos, some groceries, and a limited amount of prepared foods. These days, the store sells some 600 items, says Withanwattana, who bought it in 2011 and expanded it in 2014. Hard-to-find Thai ingredients like Nguan Soon brand ground galangal; Healthy Boy black soy sauce; and various condiments, including Pigeon brand fermented mustard greens line the shelves. A vast snack selection includes Lays potato chips in such Thai-forward flavors as *maeng ka na*, fashioned after a snack of lime, chilie, and dried shrimp wrapped in a betel leaf.

Before Withanwattana took over, Sugar Club sold a few desserts, but now it truly lives up to its name. There are more than a dozen desserts, from traditional Thai ones like mango sticky rice and toasted bread coated in sugar and drizzled with condensed milk to over-the-top toast creations involving slabs of Pullman bread drenched in rich butter and topped with ice cream and fruits. The latter includes Romeo toast, which boasts banana, Nutella, Kit Kat candies, chocolate sauce, and chocolate ice cream.

"I really love dessert," Withanwattana says. "I'm ok to not eat food. I can eat dessert for a whole day." No need for you to limit yourself to dessert at Sugar Club though. There are scores of prepared items – from soups and stews to crab meat fried rice – to take home or reheat and eat at the seating area, which doubles as a gallery for local Thai artists.

Withanwattana has come full circle since he first visited Sugar Club. These days he lives above the store with family.

Address 81-18 Broadway, Elmhurst, NY 11373, +1 (718) 565-9018, www.home.sugarclub.nyc, info@sugarclub.nyc | **Getting there** M or R train to Elmhurst Avenue | **Hours** Daily 9am–9pm | **Tip** Just down the road, you'll find the beautiful historic Reformed Church of Newtown, which was built in 1831. Be sure to check out the graveyard (85-15 Broadway, Elmhurst, NY 11373, www.rcnewtown.org).

96_ Thalia Spanish Theatre
Experience a world of Latin and Spanish culture

Lightning fast accordion runs, alternately plaintive and joyous, accompanied by strings and a piano, fill the air while couples dance the tango in 2/4 time. You're not in Argentina though, but in Sunnyside, at the Thalia Spanish Theatre, where the annual performance is one of the most popular at the borough's only Hispanic theatre, drawing tango fans from as far away as New Orleans.

The accordion player Raul Jaurena is a world-class bandoneon player, as the instrument is known in his native Uruguay. "We're very lucky to have him – he's one of the best bandoneon players in the world," says Thalia's artistic director Angel Gil Orrios. The tango performances have been taking place for 29 years and have included various interpretations, including an African spin, which added congas and substituted a marimba for the piano. "Every year we can experiment, we can take risks here because it's a small theater," Orrios says.

Thalia also plays host to other music as well as plays, comedies, and dramas. The casts of all of the plays are bilingual and they alternate English and Spanish performances. The theater, which was founded in 1977 by Cuban actress Silvia Brito, takes its name from Thalia, the Greek muse of comedy.

"She loved Spain so much that when she started it was only plays from Spain in Spanish," Orrios says. "Later on she brought flamenco." These days, Thalia has four resident dance companies representing Spanish flamenco, Mexican dance, and two Colombian companies. In true Queens fashion, the newest company, Cali Salsa Pal Mundo, is doing a production called Dances of the World that features Bollywood, Arabian belly dancing, and American rock and roll.

"What makes us unique is precisely the fact that most of what we do is world premieres or American premieres of the best writers and composers from Spain, Latin America, and Hispanics in the United States," Orrios says.

Address 41-17 Greenpoint Avenue, Sunnyside, NY 11104, +1 (718) 729-3880, www.thaliatheatre.org | Getting there 7 train to 40th Street–Lowery Street Station | Hours See website for tickets and performance schedule | Tip Continue your exploration of Hispanic culture with a stop for dinner at I Love Paraguay (43-16 Greenpoint Avenue, Sunnyside, NY 11104, www.ilovepy.com).

97__Tony Vaccaro Museum
Celebrity portraits with a plate of pasta

With MoMA PS1, the Noguchi Museum, and dozens of artists' studios, Long Island City is known as a hotbed for the arts. One of the most unique collections can't be found in a museum or a gallery, though. It's in an Italian restaurant.

You'll find Tony's Table – seating for six next to a window – in the back of Gianna Cerbone-Teoli's restaurant, Manducatis Rustica. Tony is Michelantonio Celestino Onofrio Vaccaro, a photographer who has photographed some 2,000 of the world's most famous people, from sports icons and politicians to artists and movie stars, for such magazines as *Flair*, *Look*, and *Time*. The 95-year-old photographer, who still has a studio in the neighborhood, has shot everyone from screen icons Sophia Loren and Grace Kelly to artists Pablo Picasso and Georgia O'Keeffe.

A giant photo of O'Keeffe in the Santa Fe desert, which Vaccaro shot for *Look* in 1960, hangs in the restaurant's Georgia O'Keeffe Room. "The day I opened up the restaurant, Tony came in and said, 'Oh Gianna, from one great woman to another, you must have Georgia on your wall,'" Cerbone-Teoli recalls. The same wall also features a spread of Ali McGraw from the movie *Love Story* that ran in *Look*, as well as black-and-whites of Picasso and Marcel Marceau. You'll find champion Olympic sprinter Florence "FloJo" Griffith Joyner to the right of Tony's table. By the fireplace is a photo of a young, brunette Lauren Bacall and a wistful looking Shirley MacLaine on a swing in a gauzy white shirt, her bosoms just barely visible. The bar plays hosts to political figures too: JFK and Eleanor Roosevelt. Architect Frank Lloyd Wright – hands outstretched as he describes a waterfall – graces another wall.

"I know Tony because his Uncle Beppe used to watch me when I was little," Cerbone-Teoli says. "He's been almost like a father figure – he's more family than anything else."

Address 46-35 Vernon Boulevard, Long Island City, NY 11101, +1 (718) 937-1312, www.manducatisrustica.com | Getting there 7 train to Vernon Boulevard–Jackson Avenue | Hours Tue–Fri 11am–10pm, Sat & Sun 2–10pm | Tip If you've eaten too much of Mamma Gianna's pasta, work it off at the nearby CrossFit Gantry gym (10-19 46th Road, Long Island City, NY 11101, www.crossfitgantry.com).

98__Top To Bottom
A wealth of street art styles at an LIC warehouse

In graffiti lingo, "top to bottom" refers to artwork covering the full height and width of a subway car. In the world of Queens' street art, it refers to Top to Bottom, an actual place where art covers a three-story building south of the Queensboro Bridge. Works by more than 60 artists from 14 countries – ranging from old-school New York City graffiti to photorealism – are featured.

The project's curator James P. Quinn says it took a year to complete. It's hard for him to name a favorite, but he says the Magda Love piece, a phantasmagorical landscape in bright hues, has an "intense vibrant natural language that is very transformative and exciting to bring to an industrial area." Magdalena "Magda Love" Marcenaro was born in Argentina and is one of the many artists from around the world whose works are displayed. The *Paint Machines* by Spanish artist Kans, with their green and yellow piping, adorn the building's security gates, and they are reflective of the neighborhood's industrial vibe.

With a wealth of styles and techniques before your eyes, you're sure to find something that speaks to you on the walls of the 124,000-square-foot former warehouse. Realism is represented by German artist CASE Maclaim's striking depiction of two hands and a needle being threaded with a scarlet strand. Andrea "Queen Andrea" von Bujdoss, whose work can also be seen around Astoria, has a lovely piece that combines classic graffiti lettering with a positive message and a feminine sensibility. "Go All Out!" read her bubbly pink and orange letters that frame a window.

Tucked away on the side of the building used for parking is a piece by Semz that pays tribute to the glory days of subway graffiti. Beneath its subway cars, there's a whimsical portrayal of men in suits and ties chasing down a writer as his spray paint cans fall to the ground. "This one's cool," Quinn says of the work by Bronx-based artist Yes2.

Address 43-01 21st Street, Long Island City, NY 11101, www.artsorg.nyc, artsorgnyc@gmail.com | **Getting there** E and 7 train to Court Square–23rd Street, F train to the 21st Street–Queensbridge Station | **Hours** Unrestricted | **Tip** At 21st and 40th Avenue, you can see the mural devoted to the Queensbridge Houses' favorite son, the rapper, Nas.

99 A Tribe Called Quest Mural

Pay tribute the 1980s rap pioneers

In the late 1980s, rap group A Tribe Called Quest honed their rhymes on Linden Boulevard. "Back in the days on the Boulevard of Linden / We used to kick routines and presence was fittin'," Q-Tip sang on the 1991 classic, "Check The Rhime," thus immortalizing the thoroughfare. The group filmed the song's music video on the roof of Nu-Clear Dry Cleaners on the corner of 192nd Street and Linden.

"You on point, Phife? All the time, Tip," went the classic call and response between Kamaal Ibn "Q-Tip" John Fareed and Malik "Phife Dawg" Taylor as they rapped during their packed concerts.

In 1993, Tribe once again gave a shout out to their favorite street and to Queens itself on "Steve Biko," a track named for the South African anti-apartheid activist. "Linden Boulevard represent, represent," Phife sang, answered by Q-Tip: "Tribe Called Quest represent, represent / Queens is in the house represent, represent."

These days, the Boulevard of Linden is home to a mural that commemorates Tribe's influence on hip-hop. You'll find it on the wall of the same Nu-Clear Dry Cleaners. Painted by artist Vincent Ballentine, it features a red, black, and green Afrocentric color scheme that echoes those used on the group's album covers. It bears the words, "Represent, Represent," along with portraits of Q-Tip, Ali Shaheed Muhammad, Jarobi White, and Phife Dawg.

Ballentine painted it in the summer 2016, a few months after Phife Dawg died from complications of diabetes at the age of 45. "Phife came from the golden era when hip-hop was something to be cherished. Him passing leaves another gap that will never be filled again," Vallentine said. "As an artist, it's my job never to let that memory die and represent, represent."

Don't miss the sign for Malik 'Phife Dawg' Taylor Way.

Address 192-10 Linden Boulevard, St. Albans, NY 11412 | Getting there E train to Jamaica Center–Parsons/Archer then Q4 bus to Linden Boulevard and 192nd Street | Hours Unrestricted | Tip Naida Nelson Njoku's Maria Rose International Doll House sells beautiful and ethnically diverse dolls sporting kente cloth, lederhosen and kimonos (115-42 173rd Street, St. Albans, NY 11412, by appointment through Shirley Phipps, +1 (917) 817-8653).

100_ TV Lounge

Kick back 1960s-style and enjoy classic cartoons

It's only fitting that the Museum of The Moving Image should be situated around the corner from historic film production facility Kaufman Astoria Studios. It contains thousands of objects, from early motion picture cameras to movie memorabilia, that chronicle the history not only of motion picture production but of television and other visual media, including virtual reality goggles.

Across from an arcade with dozens of vintage video games ranging from Pong and Computer Space to Frogger and Donkey Kong, you'll find a groovy 12-foot cube devoted to another childhood pastime: watching Saturday morning cartoons. Jim Isermann's TV lounge features psychedelic yellow-and-orange op-art hangings and a black-and-white cowhide sectional worthy of Austin Powers and, of course, a television playing cartoons.

As comfortable as the plastic slip-covered couches are, the best place for your small set to take in the show might just be the pink shag carpet. Isermann's creation channels the vibe of a 1960s suburban rec room so much that you might forget you are in a museum and expect your mother to emerge with a pitcher of Kool-Aid and a tray of snacks. It's a tableau that Isermann himself, who was born in Kenosha, Wisconsin in 1955, might well have enjoyed growing up.

Even though the room itself is pure 1960s, the show on the set – "Spider-Man and His Amazing Friends" – dates to 1981. "Spidey Goes Hollywood" details the superhero's experience with the moving image-making of his own as he makes a movie with hapless mustachioed director, Stan Blockbuster, who bears a passing resemblance to Spider-Man's creator Stan Lee.

The wise-cracking web slinger Spider-Man, also known as Peter Parker, comes from Queens where he attended Forest Hills High School, along with the real-life Ramones. No doubt that's why the curators chose to show *Spider-Man and His Amazing Friends*.

Address 36-01 35th Avenue, Astoria, NY 11106, +1 (718) 777-6800, www.movingimage.us, info@movingimage.us | **Getting there** R train to Steinway Street | **Hours** Wed & Thu 10:30am–5pm, Fri 10:30am–8pm (free admission 4–8pm), Sat & Sun 10:30am–6pm | **Tip** In Jackson Heights, you'll find another tribute to Queens' most famous superhero. The "Queens is The Future" mural on the handball court of I.S. 145 features Spider-Man lifting up a subway car (33-34 80th Street, Jackson Heights, NY 11372).

101__Uke Hut

The sounds of the islands...in Astoria

The ukulele is most often associated with Hawaii and tiki culture, yet Queens, Astoria to be specific, has become a stronghold of ukulele culture thanks to Ken Bari Murray's shop, Uke Hut. The local musician fell in love with the instrument while living in Hawaii and opened the shop on Halloween 2015. Not only does Uke Hut have the distinction of being the only ukulele store in Queens, it's the only such emporium on the East Coast. More than 200 ukuleles in all shapes and sizes line the walls of the Astoria shop, from colorful toy plastic Makalas that sell for $52, to glossy collectors' pieces made from gorgeous acacia and koa woods that fetch $1,000 or more.

There are pineapple-shaped ukuleles, electric slide ukuleles, concert, tenor, baritone, and soprano varieties. The shop also offers some hybrids, like the guitalele and banjolele. Japanese ukulele master Sakai Masafumi, who minds the store on Tuesdays and Wednesdays, is more than happy to tell you all about Hawaii's favorite four-string instrument. Don't be surprised if he places the instrument nicknamed the "Jumping Flea" in your hands and teaches you how to play some chords. If you find yourself catching the ukulele bug after your visit, the store offers private lessons. More accomplished players can get their ukuleles repaired at the shop too.

Every Saturday night starting at 8:08pm – a tip of the hat to Hawaii's area code – Masafumi performs a concert. Come early for sound check and get an opportunity to play a ukulele for yourself. Or better yet, join in on the "Bring Your Uke Night" jam session held every Friday at 7:30pm. The shop plays host to a half-dozen ukulele enthusiasts of varying skill levels who join together to play everything, including Jimmy Buffet tunes, Beatles songs, Motown favorites, and folk music ranging from Aiko Aiko to Irish ballads, like "Red is the Rose."

Address 36-01 36th Avenue, Astoria, NY 11106, +1 (929) 500-8680, www.ukehut.com |
Getting there E, M, or R train to 36th Street | Hours Daily noon–7pm | Tip You may not
be able to surf near Uke Hut, but why not take a dip at nearby Astoria Pool? 80 years after
it first opened, with majestic views of the Triborough Bridge, it is still the largest public
pool in New York City (19th St & 23rd Drive, Astoria, NY 11105, www.nycgovparks.org/
parks/astoria-park/facilities/outdoor-pools/astoria-pool).

102 United Sherpa Association Buddhist Monastery

Trek to NYC's cradle of Nepalese Buddhist culture

Just off Broadway sits a red brick church adorned with yellow, green, red, white, and blue penants. The former St. Matthew's Church was built in 1947, but these days it's a Buddhist temple run by the United Sherpa Association, which bought the building in 2011.

It's hard to believe the bright red doors framed with red columns and dozens of auspicious Buddhist symbols are the original doors, but they are. The most important of these icons, the *dharmachakra* – a spoked, multihued wheel with swirls of blue, green, and red – sits in the center flanked by two deer. The deer represent the place where Buddha gave his first teaching, according to the association's president, Urgen Sherpa. "This is the entrance to the deer park," Sherpa says, gesturing to the doors. "It means Buddha's teaching is going on here."

Doff your shoes and enter the inner sanctum where multihued cylindrical banners known as *duk* hang from the ceiling and a dozen *thangka*, or holy tapestries adorn the walls. Among the figures depicted is the founder of Tibetan Buddhism, Padmasambhava, known as Guru Rinpoche. Several majestic gold statues are enshrined on the altar. In the center is Shakyamuni Buddha, the historical Buddha, who was born in Nepal. He is flanked by Avalokiteśvara, the bodhisattva of compassion on the left and Guru Rinpoche on the right.

"That is the person we call the second Buddha," Sherpa says. "He is the one who brought Buddhism into Tibet in the 7th century." While Elmhurst is home to the most Sherpa people to be found outside of Nepal and many who worship at the temple are Sherpa, other Nepali ethnicities, including Thakalis and Newari, come to the temple too. Indians, Bangladeshi, and Burmese also come, Sherpa says. And now you are welcome too.

Address 41-01 75th Street, Queens Elmhurst, NY 11373, +1(718) 779-7300 | Getting there 7, E, F, M, or R train to Jackson Heights–Roosevelt Avenue | Hours Daily 10am–6pm | Tip Continue your exploration into South Asian Buddhist culture with a visit to the Sri Lankan New York Buddhist Vihara (214-22 Spencer Avenue, Queens Village, NY 11427, +1 (718) 468-4262, www.nybv.us/nybv).

103__ Vander Ende-Onderdonk House

Our Dutch colonial past in industrial Ridgewood

When New York City's oldest Dutch Colonial stone house was built in 1709, Newtown Creek flowed nearby, and the now gritty industrial streets were home to farms. For hundreds of years, the Vander Ende-Onderdonk House and neighboring Woodward Farm ferried produce to New Amsterdam. This last remnant of local Dutch history sits across from a meat packing plant near the Brooklyn / Queens border.

"They tore down all the houses that were easy to knock down," says curator Richard Asbell. "These walls are two-and-a-half-foot-thick field stone." The stones are so named because farmers would find them while tending the fields and then use them to build foundations.

"The very rich Dutch farmers could afford heat," Asbell says of Paulus Vander Ende, who built the house, and Adrian Onderdonk, who owned it for much of the 19th century. In summer, Dutch doors (the top half opens, and the bottom stays closed to keep animals out) at either end of the house would be opened, allowing a cooling breeze to blow through.

Today, the house is a museum with artifacts unearthed on the property. Clay pipes and a 19th-century English platter reassembled from shards of glazed ceramic are among the curios displayed. Don't miss St. Nicholas Day on December 4. During the Dutch Christmas celebration, St. Nicholas, outfitted with a miter and staff, hands out gifts to children. The house is bathed in candlelight and holds a Christmas feast at night.

Were it not for the Greater Ridgewood Historical Society, this piece of history would have gone the way of its neighbors. In the 1970s, after a fire, the Vander Ende-Onderdonk House was to be demolished. Thanks to the Society's efforts, it was listed on the National Register of Historic Places in 1977.

Address 18-20 Flushing Avenue, Ridgewood, NY 11385, +1 (718) 456-1776, www.onderdonkhouse.org | **Getting there** L train to Jefferson Street Station | **Hours** Sat 1–4pm, Sun noon–4pm | **Tip** Continue your exploration of the neighborhood with a walk through the Central Ridgewood Historic District, where you'll find the Joseph Meyerrose House and other classic residences built by German American immigrants in the early 20th century (66-75 Forest Avenue, Ridgewood, NY 11385).

104 Venditti Square

Mafia murder in Ridgewood's once mean streets

"Down these mean streets a man must go who is himself not mean; who is neither tarnished, nor afraid," reads a quote from detective writer Raymond Chandler on a plaque dedicated to New York City Police Department Detective Anthony J. Venditti, who was shot dead by Genovese family mobsters on January 21, 1986. You'll find it in Venditti Square in Ridgewood, not far from the site of the brutal murder, which took place at the intersection of St. Nicholas and Myrtle Avenues.

Today the streets – filled with businesses like Nick's Barber Shop and La Botanica Abebe Oshun – are anything but mean. That wasn't the case on that winter evening in 1986, when Detective Venditti and his partner Detective Kathleen Burke were tailing Federico "Fritzy" Giovanelli, a member of the Genovese organized crime family, who operated a gambling ring out of the nearby Bushwick Democratic Club. As Detective Venditti left Castillo's Diner at Myrtle and St. Nicholas, he was surrounded by three men. His partner, who had circled the block while he used the diner's men's room, approached when she saw Venditti pinned against the wall. Soon thereafter she was shot in the chest, and Venditti was shot fatally, twice in the right side of the face.

Giovanelli, who was seen fleeing the scene, was arrested with Genovese crime family members Carmine Gualtiere and Steve Maltese. After three state trials and numerous jury deadlocks, all three men were acquitted of murder, although they were later convicted of racketeering.

"The only thing that I think that might have bothered him is that this is truly a cold case," Patricia Venditti, his widow said in a memorial service on the 30th anniversary of her husband's death. "That gave anguish to his mother all these years."

Today, the Bushwick Democratic Club is long gone, and the diner has changed hands, but Venditti's memory lives on in the square.

Address 54–31 Myrtle Avenue, Ridgewood, NY 11385 | Getting there L train to Myrtle–Wyckoff Avenues | Hours Accessible 24 hours | Tip Mafioso John "The Teflon Don" Gotti used to do business out of the Bergin Hunt and Fish Club in Ozone Park. Today, the former social club houses a medical supply business and a pet groomer (98-04 101st Avenue, Ozone Park, NY 11416).

105__ Voelker Orth Museum & Garden

A fragrant window into Flushing's past

It's hard to believe that the traffic that now zooms down Northern Boulevard was once limited to horse-drawn carriages. Yet as you can see from a photo on the wall of The Voelker Orth Museum Bird Sanctuary and Victorian Garden, it's true. Tucked just off Northern, the garden has more than 100 varieties of flowers, including fragrant pink viburnum that lines the fence outside. The house has been restored to look as it would have when it was purchased in 1899 by a German immigrant family.

Today the house is done up in pink and white shingles. Old family photos were instrumental in the restoration, and many family photos are on view in the house, which also features the family piano and a library lined with volumes of inspirational poetry.

Back when the Voelkers lived there, the lawn was the site of social gatherings. These days, it's the setting for summertime Shakespeare plays. Victorian gardens often featured apiaries. In keeping with this, Voelker Orth has a beehive. Its honey routinely wins first or second prize in the Queens County Fair.

Heirloom roses were also a common feature of the Victorian garden. A pink heirloom, known as the Queen Elizabeth, graces the space in the museum's bay window. Elizabeth Orth, whose grandfather, Conrad Voelker, purchased the property, grew the very same variety of roses in the same place.

Late in life, Orth wrote a will specifying she wanted the property to become a museum. "She gave us this name, the Voelker Orth Museum Bird Sanctuary and Victorian Garden," Deborah Silverfine says. "She gave us very few directives." One of those very few directives was that there would be weddings on the site. It's especially romantic since Elizabeth herself never married.

Address 149-19 38th Avenue, Flushing, NY 11354, +1 (718) 359-6227, www.vomuseum.org | Getting there Long Island Railroad to Murray Hill Station or 7 train to Flushing–Main Street, then Q15A bus to 150th Street/Northern Boulevard | Hours Tue, Sat & Sun 1–4pm; calling in advance to confirm | Tip Built in 1862, the nearby Flushing Town Hall offers another window into the neighborhood's past and today features everything from jazz and puppet shows to classical music and spoken word (137-35 Northern Boulevard, Flushing, NY 11354, +1 (718) 463-7700, www.flushingtownhall.org).

106_ Wat Buddha Thai Thavorn Vanaram

A Buddhist temple in an urban jungle

At first glance, it's possible to mistake Wat Buddha Thai Thavorn Vanaram, a temple serving Elmhurst's Thai community, for an apartment building. A closer look, however, reveals Thai flags and an ornate entrance surmounted by a yellow-and-red structure supported by columns topped with sacred birds.

Around the back of the temple, the grounds feature statues more common in Southeast Asia than Central Queens: a gigantic reclining Buddha and Huang Po To, a Thai Buddhist master who lived in the 1800s. Huang Po To is in seated posture flanked by vases of pink flowers and adorned with a yellow-and-red floral garland.

Huang Po To is one of many things – including people – that are splashed with water during Song Kran, or Thai New Year, which falls on April 13 each year. The temple holds a festival on the following Sunday. It's not unusual to see monks clad in saffron-colored robes with water guns and buckets splashing the guests. In fact, to be so anointed is a sign of good luck. Hundreds of people from the surrounding community gather to enjoy New York City's largest free Thai buffet, which features some of the most exquisite Thai food to be found in Queens.

Much of the food served at Song Kran comes from Isaan in Thailand's northeast, just like the temple's abbot, Pramaha Thawin Pukhao. Wat Buddha Thai Thavorn Vanaram is named for Pukhao's master, Han Po Thavorn. *Vanaram* denotes "in the forest."

Enshrined in the temple's top-most chamber is the Emerald Buddha. This golden-crowned Buddha looks much like its counterpart in Bangkok's Grand Palace. "It's the only other one outside of Thailand," Pukhao says. "You have to get permission from the King, and we brought the Emerald Buddha to the King's palace to be blessed."

Address 76-16 46th Avenue, Elmhurst, NY 11373, +1 (718) 803-9881 | **Getting there** 7, E, F, M, or R train to Jackson Heights–Roosevelt Avenue, turn left onto Broadway, turn right onto 76th Street, turn left onto 46th Avenue | **Hours** Daily 7am–8pm | **Tip** On weekends from 1pm to 5pm, chef Cherry and her crew serve up steaming bowls of Thai boat noodle soup at Pata Paplean (76-21 Woodside Avenue, Elmhurst).

107__Welling Court Mural Project

A rotating showcase of street art hidden in Astoria

Astoria is known for its art museums, including the Socrates Sculpture Park and the Noguchi Museum. But one of the neighborhood's most unique destinations for art can be found on dozens of roll-down gates and walls instead of museum walls. Welling Court Mural Project, a rotating showcase for global street art, began in 2009.

Neighborhood resident Jonathan Ellis connected with Ad Hoc Art in an effort to improve the neighborhood's bland industrial streetscape. The first mural was painted in December 2009 by Polish artist M-City in the dead of winter. "Poland is crazy cold. This is easy," the artist said of his painting the 120-foot wall over three days. The following May, the first-ever Welling Court Mural Project took place with 44 artists.

Every year on the second Saturday of June, Ad Hoc Art and Welling Court Mural Project play host to an all-day block party as the year's crop of artists put up their works. The event draws people from the local community and all over the world.

These days, Welling Court features artists from many different countries, including Central and South America, Eastern Europe, and Japan. "We pretty much have all the continents represented except Antarctica," said Garrison Buxton, Director of Ad Hoc Art.

The project features more than 120 works of art ranging from wild-style graffiti to whimsical pieces depicting pop culture tropes like robots, as well as political commentary addressing women's and gay rights and free speech. Style and techniques include brushwork, aerosol, yarn bombing, and sculpture. "We have everything from classic graffiti originators to contemporary artists," Buxton said. "If you can't find something you like, then you don't like public art."

The best way to explore? Get lost amid the murals.

"RE REALLY IS NO
E LEVEL OF LEAD."
PHYSICIAN,
LINT, MICHIGAN.

KATIE YAMASAKI
CALEB NEELON.
2016

Address 12th Street and Astoria Boulevard, www.adhocart.org/site/category/welling-court, info@adhocart.org | **Getting there** W train to 30th Avenue, walk northeast on 31st Street, make a left onto 30th Avenue and a slight left onto Welling Court; N train to Astoria–Ditmars Boulevard, walk south toward 31st Street, turn right onto 31st Street, turn right onto Astoria Boulevard, turn left onto 12th Street, turn right onto Welling Court | **Hours** Unrestricted | **Tip** Straddling the border of East Elmhurst and Astoria is the picturesque Lent-Riker-Smith Homestead, New York City's oldest home. Built in 1656, it is named for the same Rikers as the prison. In the backyard is a graveyard where 132 members of the family are buried (78-03 19th Road, East Elmhurst, NY 11370, www.rikerhome.com).

108__Whispering Column of Jerash

Ancient Roman relic, a gift from a king

An ancient relic that predates Flushing Meadows–Corona Park by 2000 years sits on the edge of a grove of trees across from a soccer field. How did a 30-foot-high marble Roman column topped with an elaborate scrollwork wind up in Queens? After all, the Roman Empire never extended to the World's Borough.

This antiquity, known as the *Whispering Column of Jerash*, was part of the 1964–1965 World's Fair, which took place in the park and themed, "Man in a Shrinking Globe in an Expanding Universe."

The column was donated to the City of New York by Jordan's King Hussein. During the fair, it stood outside that country's pavilion, which featured another ancient relic of no small import, one of the Dead Sea Scrolls.

"My country will not be able to exhibit atomic power, or a special mechanical energy, or an advanced electrical device, but we will be quite able to exhibit that which shall remain when everything else shall vanish," said King Hussein at the pavilion's unveiling for the fair. "In our pavilion, the oldest Torah; the Church of the Nativity, and the Mosque of the Dome of the Rock, shall stand symbols of righteousness, tolerance, peace and brotherhood."

The column was first erected in 120 AD by the Romans in the ancient city of Jerash, which at the time was part of the Roman Empire. It was thought to be part of a whispering gallery of columns at Temple of Artemis. Recent archeological research reveals that the column cannot be from that temple given its size and construction.

Today, the only whispering happening around the second oldest outdoor antiquity in New York City after Cleopatra's Needle in Central Park is that of the trees. With the Unisphere in the background, the Whispering Column of Jerash stands as testament to history.

Address Flushing Meadows–Corona Park | **Getting there** 7 train to 111th Street in Queens. From the Unisphere in the park, follow the broad promenade until you reach the *Rocket Thrower* and turn right. You'll see a soccer field on the left; the Column will be on the right in the grove of trees. | **Hours** Unrestricted | **Tip** East of the Unisphere, you'll find another World's Fair relic: the Vatican Pavilion Exedra. This semicircular granite bench marks the site that was once the Vatican Pavilion. It is also site of Virgin Mary apparitions seen by Veronica Lueken of Bayside, and it continues to draw the faithful on Sunday mornings.

109__Willets Point

Explore the Iron Triangle before it rusts away

Across from Citi Field, you'll find potholed streets lined with body shops, salvage yards, muffler specialists, and mechanics where discarded work boots hang from telephone wires. Known as the Iron Triangle, Willets Point has been home to salvage yards since before Shea Stadium, Citi Field's forerunner, was built.

This junkyard is as diverse as Queens itself. Dominican mechanics enjoy a game of dominoes while *cumbia* music plays from the neighboring Ecuadorean shop. Adding to the flavor is the House of Spices, America's largest manufacturer of Indian foods.

"There's an Israeli salvage yard across the street, next to an Afghan muffler shop, which is next door to a Peruvian deli," says Sam Sambucci, whose family has been in the auto salvage business since before Shea.

Look south and you can make out the Observation Towers from the 1964 World's Fair. Before Robert Moses transformed it, the site inspired the Valley of Ashes in *The Great Gatsby*.

Moses tried to annex Willets Point, a "Valley of Iron," as part of his World's Fair plans, but the neighborhood successfully fought him with the help of a young lawyer named Mario Cuomo.

In 2006, the city took up plans again for redevelopment, razing a good chunk of the triangle on 126th Street between Roosevelt and 38th Avenues. "I'd rather be sitting in a nice office like I used to be around the block at Sambucci Bros. That's all destroyed now, just a flat piece of property," Sambucci says.

Sambucci's specialty is German cars from Mercedes, Audi, and Volkswagen. "Every day I drive a Ford Expedition; it's the only way I can get in here, but my night car is a BMW M5."

In 2013, British artist Banksy placed a replica of the Great Sphinx outside Bernardo Veles' shop. A worker took it and has yet to sell it. "You should have taken the $50,000," Sambucci joshed his pal.

Address Bounded by Northern Boulevard to the north, 126th Street and Citi Field to the west, Roosevelt Avenue and Flushing Meadows–Corona Park to the south, and the Flushing River to the east. | **Getting there** 7 train to Mets–Willets Point | **Hours** Accessible 24 hours | **Tip** The nearby World's Fair Marina features a waterside promenade that runs all the way from LaGuardia Airport to Whitestone and is perfect for biking or walking (1 Flushing Bay Promenade, East Elmhurst, NY 11369, www.nycgovparks.org/facilities/marinas/13).

110 Zapatería Mexico

For all your mariachi and Mexican cowboy needs

You'll find this shop, whose name literally means "Mexican shoe store," in the heart of Jackson Heights. The 20-year-old emporium stocks much more than shoes though. While it does carry *huaraches*, Jorge Orduña's shop is really an outfitter for *vaqueros*, or Mexican cowboys, and mariachi musicians.

Orduña, who hails from Coatzingo, Mexico, opened the shop when he noticed his compatriots had traded in *botas* for sneakers. Zapatería Mexicana was just a shoe store in a basement. Eventually Orduña moved to the larger location and began to add more merchandise, including the clothing, which he imports from Guadalajara.

Pointy-toed Mexican boots, or *tribales*, line the front display windows. Zapatería Mexico's hundreds of *botas* are fashioned from such exotic materials as ostrich and alligator, as well as cowhide. Orduña imports the stippled ostrich boots in every shade of tan and brown, as well as lavender and aqua, from León, a city known for leather goods.

Just inside the door are several broad-brimmed mariachi-style sombreros in silver, gold, blue, purple, and magenta. There's even one decorated in the colors of the Mexican flag. These hats retail for $45, as does a large straw sombrero that reads "Viva Mexico." Cowboy hats come in many styles, including a vented number known as the Coyote, which sells for $45. Striving to be a bad *hombre*? Then Gomher is your brand.

A stack of $120 premium *vaquero* hats signed by the members of popular Norteño group Los Creadorez sits on the counter. They're not the only Mexican Norteño musicians to shop here either. It's no surprise that Los Tigres del Norte have visited too, given that the shop has everything you need to look like a Mexican musician, including tailored suits and shirts.

Not up for buying an entire mariachi outfit or boots? Don't worry – you can always take home a miniature mariachi sombrero for $5.

Address 88-07 Roosevelt Avenue, Jackson Heights, NY 11372, +1 (718) 899-1742, www.zapateriamexico.com | Getting there 7 train to 90th Street–Elmhurst Avenue | Hours Daily 9am–9pm | Tip Manuel de Dios Unanue Triangle honors the Cuban journalist of the same name who reported extensively about local Colombian drug traffickers in the late 1980s and early 1990s. He was gunned down in Queens while dining at a nearby restaurant on March 11, 1992 (Baxter and Roosevelt Avenues and Manuel de Dios Unanue Street, Elmhurst, NY 11373).

111_ Zombie Gnome Bench

A tribute to Charles Bukowski, and, well, you

Just off the corner of 11th Street and 47th Road is one of the most whimsical houses in Long Island City. At first glance, the two-story home looks like any other domicile on the block. Just to the right of the royal blue door though sits a bench on a platform of artificial grass surrounded by several cavorting garden gnomes and other statues.

"You are marvelous. The gods await to delight in you," reads an inscription carved into the green bench, leaving no doubt that passersby are indeed invited to sit. Grab a seat and you'll notice another component to this artistic streetscape, a lamppost done up in blue mosaic tiles topped by a sunflower. "There are always people out there on the bench," says the home's owner, Chris Carlson. "One day a nanny was doing yoga on the bench – upside down handstands."

Carlson started the project shortly after he purchased the property, which came with a couple of garden gnomes. He added some more and then the bench, which he originally intended to sneak into a park for his wife. Instead he placed it front of the house with his gnomes.

The fanciful tableau's rotating cast of characters now includes 10 gnomes and several "Where the Wild Things Are" figures. "Mark Twain is out there, and Edgar Allen Poe. Anybody I like is out there," Carlson says. The zombies come out around Halloween time. "I had these two devil lady mannequins out there for Halloween once, but my wife said, 'There's got to be a limit.'"

He plans to add photos of other people he likes, including Mr. T and Pee Wee Herman, to the lamppost and might even top it off with a 4-foot garden gnome. "It's a constant project," he said, adding that his neighbors are fine with his zany labor of love.

The quote on the bench comes from the poet Charles Bukowski. "It's shocking that it's from him because most of his stuff is just depressing," Carlson says.

You are marvelous. The gods wait to delight in you

Address 10-50 47th Road, Long Island City, NY 11101 | Getting there 7 train to Vernon Boulevard–Jackson Avenue | Hours Visible from the outside only | Tip Stop in the nearby beer hall Bierocracy for a cold glass of Czech pilsener and a snack (12–23 Jackson Avenue, Long Island City, NY 11101, www.bierocracy.com).

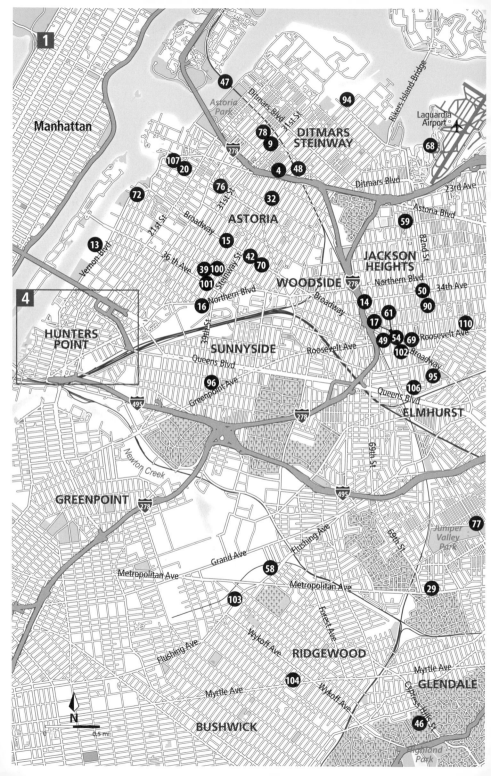

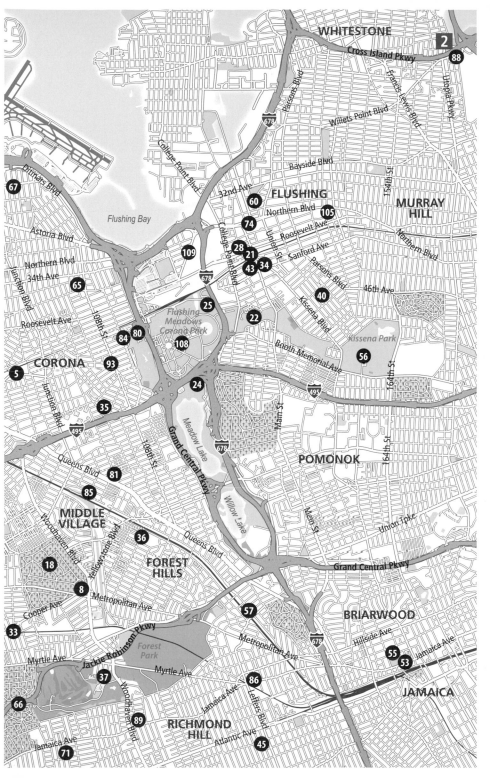

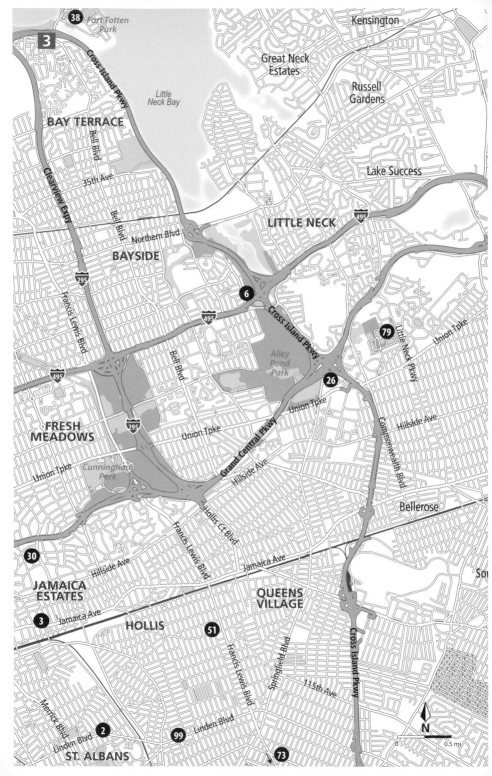

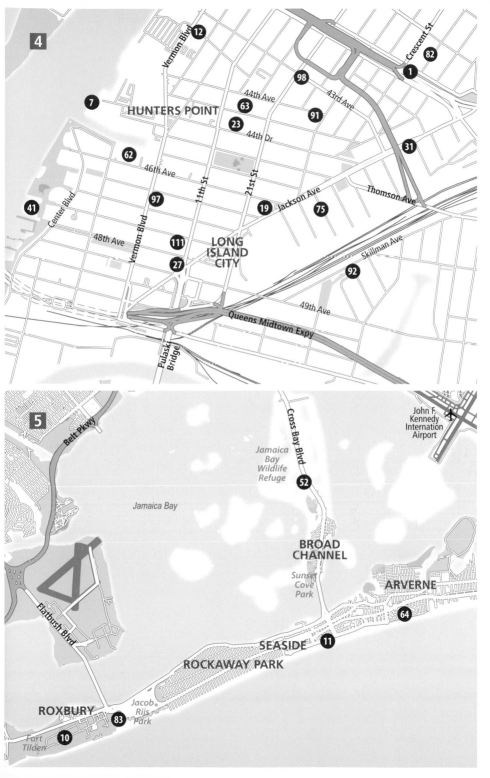

Floriana Petersen, Steve Werney
**111 PLACES IN SAN
FRANCISCO THAT YOU
MUST NOT MISS**
ISBN 978-3-95451-609-4

Jo-Anne Elikann
**111 PLACES IN NEW YORK
THAT YOU MUST NOT MISS**
ISBN 978-3-95451-052-8

Allison Robicelli, John Dean
**111 PLACES IN BALTIMORE
THAT YOU MUST NOT MISS**
ISBN 978-3-7408-0158-8

Laurel Moglen, Julia Posey
**111 PLACES IN LOS ANGELES
THAT YOU SHOULDN'T MISS**
ISBN 978-3-95451-884-5

Amy Bizzarri, Susie Inverso
**111 PLACES IN CHICAGO
THAT YOU MUST NOT MISS**
ISBN 978-3-7408-0156-4

Mark Gabor, Susan Lusk
**111 Shops in New York
That You Must Not Miss**
ISBN 978-3-95451-351-2

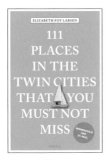

Elisabeth Larsen
**111 PLACES IN THE
TWIN CITIES THAT
YOU MUST NOT MISS**
ISBN 978-3-7408-0029-1

Desa Philadelphia
**111 SHOPS IN LOS ANGELES
THAT YOU MUST NOT MISS**
ISBN 978-3-95451-615-5

Gordon Streisand
**111 PLACES IN MIAMI
AND THE KEYS
THAT YOU MUST NOT MISS**
ISBN 978-3-95451-644-5

Michael Murphy, Sall Asher
**111 PLACES IN NEW ORLEANS
THAT YOU MUST NOT MISS**
ISBN 978-3-95451-645-2

Petra Sophia Zimmermann
**111 PLACES IN VERONA
AND LAKE GARDA THAT
YOU MUST NOT MISS**
ISBN 978-3-95451-611-7

Rüdiger Liedtke,
Laszlo Trankovits
**111 PLACES IN CAPE TOWN
THAT YOU MUST NOT MISS**
ISBN 978-3-95451 610-0

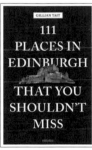

Gillian Tait
**111 PLACES IN EDINBURGH
THAT YOU SHOULDN'T MISS**
ISBN 978-3-95451-883-8

Rike Wolf
**111 PLACES IN HAMBURG
THAT YOU SHOULDN'T MISS**
ISBN 978-3-95451-234-8

Giulia Castelli Gattinara,
Mario Verin
**111 PLACES IN MILAN
THAT YOU MUST NOT MISS**
ISBN 978-3-95451-331-4

John Sykes
**111 PLACES IN LONDON
THAT YOU SHOULDN'T MISS**
ISBN 978-3-95451-346-8

Julian Treuherz,
Peter de Figueiredo
**111 PLACES IN LIVERPOOL
THAT YOU SHOULDN'T MISS**
ISBN 978-3-95451-769-5

Rüdiger Liedtke
**111 PLACES IN MUNICH
THAT YOU SHOULDN'T MISS**
ISBN 978-3-95451-222-5

Matěj Černý, Marie Peřinová
**111 PLACES IN PRAGUE
THAT YOU SHOULDN'T MISS**
ISBN 978-3-7408-0144-1

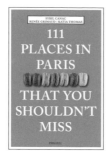

Sybil Canac, Renée Grimaud,
Katia Thomas
**111 PLACES IN PARIS THAT
YOU SHOULDN'T MISS**
ISBN 978-3-7408-0159-5

Chris Titley
**111 PLACES IN YORK THAT
YOU SHOULDN'T MISS**
ISBN 978-3-95451-768-8

Kathrin Bielfeldt,
Raymond Wong, Jürgen Bürger
**111 PLACES IN HONG KONG
THAT YOU SHOULDN'T MISS**
ISBN 978-3-95451-936-1

Justin Postlethwaite
**111 PLACES IN BATH THAT
YOU SHOULDN'T MISS**
ISBN 978-3-7408-0146-5

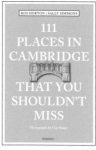

Rosalind Horton,
Sally Simmons, Guy Snape
**111 PLACES IN CAMBRIDGE
THAT YOU SHOULDN'T MISS**
ISBN 978-3-7408-0147-2

Frank McNally
**111 PLACES IN DUBLIN
THAT YOU SHOULDN'T MISS**
ISBN 978-3-95451-649-0

Gerd Wolfgang Sievers
**111 PLACES IN VENICE
THAT YOU MUST NOT MISS**
ISBN 978-3-95451-460-1

Sharon Fernandes
**111 PLACES IN NEW DELHI
THAT YOU MUST NOT MISS**
ISBN 978-3-95451-648-3

Acknowledgements

Queens is a mighty borough with many stories to tell. It is with heartfelt appreciation that I thank my editor Karen Seiger and the rest of the team at Emons for giving me the opportunity to relate these stories.

Jack Eichenbaum, Mitch Waxman, John Choe, Connie Murray, and Rob Mackay have all provided invaluable insight into the borough's history as well as much needed encouragement. Anthony Bourdain remains an inspiration, and I have fond memories of taking him to Flushing's Golden Shopping Mall. And thanks to Laurie Woolever, a powerhouse of a food writer, who not coincidentally lives in Jackson Heights. Even though he calls Minneapolis home, Andrew Zimmern has long been a champion of Queens and an inspiration in more ways than one. To my friends and family – those of you who either helped me get to some of the locations and/or endured my waxing rhapsodic about same – thank you.

Throughout the process Sami Toujani has kept me well caffeinated with the best damn cold brew on Queens Boulevard. To the Ramones up in punk rock heaven whose mural I pass every day, thanks for watching over me.

Most of all though I'd like to thank the people of Queens: inventors and innovators, cabbies and cooks, monks and gangsters, bocce players and cricket batsmen, without whom none of this would have been possible.   J.D.

I owe everything to the women in my life: To my sister Sheena Williams for joining me week after week on my adventures around Queens. I literally couldn't have done this without you. To Sonia Williams, Pat Nembhard, and Heather Williams for always cheering me on, and of course, to Tammi Williams, without whose support, I'd still be trudging through the corporate world. Finally, thanks so much to Karen Seiger for bringing me onto this project – my biggest yet! I appreciate your faith in my work.   C.W.

The Author

Queens-based food writer, culinary tour guide, and champion of Queens **Joe DiStefano** has been exploring the borough's diverse global cuisines and cultures for many years. An intrepid eater, Joe is widely recognized by such culinary luminaries as Andrew Zimmern as a go-to source on the borough's rich tapestry of cuisines and cultures, from Michelin-starred temples of gastronomy to Thai and Hindu temples where food is served. He is the founder and publisher of the Queenscentric food blog CHOPSTICKS & MARROW, and a co-founder of New York Epicurean Events and Queens Dinner Club. His work has appeared in The New York Times, Gourmet, Food Republic, and Serious Eats. His clients include Starbucks, the Boys Club of New York, Hormel, The Food Group, and Next Restaurant.

The Photographer

Born in Queens, raised in Brooklyn, **Clay Williams** is a lifelong New Yorker who photographs food, drinks and events for The New York Times, Edible Communities magazines, and the James Beard Foundation. With his camera in tow, Clay has hung on to the back of food trucks in Paris, trudged through farms in Argentina, and squeezed into tiny kitchens with world famous chefs. When he's not documenting the food system, he's at home, cooking dishes inspired by what he photographs every day. Clay lives in Sunset Park, Brooklyn, with his wife Tammi, a fellow New York native.